Irish

PHRASEBOOK

D0813042

Irish

PHRASEBOOK

MERCIER PRESS
Irish Publisher – Irish Story

Published 2017 by Mercier Press, Cork, www.mercierpress.ie,
by arrangement with Geddes & Grosset, an imprint of
The Gresham Publishing Company Ltd, Academy Park,
Building 4000, Gower Street, Glasgow, G51 1PR, Scotland.

Text written by Niall Callan
Edited by Ciarán Ó Pronntaigh
Additional material, 2014, by Martina Maher

ISBN 978 1 78117 494 4

Printed and bound in the EU

CONTENTS

CONTENTS

7

ABOUT THE IRISH LANGUAGE

Irish Gaelic, or Gaeilge, is one of the oldest surviving languages in Europe. Written sources date back to the early Christian period when scribes writing Latin manuscripts in the 6th and 7th centuries AD would annotate the margins of these documents in Irish. Other written sources include Ogham, a simplified alphabet of the early Irish language, consisting of a system of strokes and dots to represent letters. Ogham was inscribed on upright stones, most of which have been dated around the 5th and 6th centuries. These inscriptions generally consist of a person's name, possibly as a memorial or boundary marker. Hundreds of these inscribed stones survive in Ireland and are worth visiting. We can assume this written language was also documented on parchment and wood but that these materials have not survived the centuries as rock does.

Irish was spoken before these written records appear and is thought to have reached Ireland somewhere around the year 500 BC. Irish is a Celtic language like Scottish Gaelic, Welsh and Breton. Up until the 16th century, Irish and Scottish Gaelic shared a standard written language. As the two languages continued to move apart, becoming less mutually intelligible, two different written forms were adopted. Welsh and Breton, while belonging to the same family are less closely related to Irish.

In the late 19th century, various factors were to lead to the decline of Irish as the language of the majority of the population. Before the Irish famine (1845–1849) the population stood at 8.5 million. Within five years it had fallen by a quarter, and it was to fall to an all-time low figure of just over 4 million by the early 20th century. This was devastating to the country; and it also had a devastating effect on the numbers speaking Irish.

Today, about 1.77 million people throughout the whole country claim to be able to speak Irish, although 2011 census figures also show that only 77,185 use it on a daily basis. Irish speaking areas are known as *Gaeltachts,* although every city and large town will have its own Irish language schools and an Irish-speaking community.

The Gaeltacht

The term *Gaeltacht* (pronounced Gayle-tokht) is used to describe a part of Ireland where Irish is the daily language of most of the people. In the Gaeltachts, you will hear the language spoken on the streets, in the shops and in the pubs. While Irish is officially the first language of the Republic of Ireland, the Gaeltachts are areas where this is a reality, and children are raised speaking Irish before English. Several thousand Irish schoolchildren are sent to these places every year to immerse themselves in the language and to learn to speak it more fluently. That said, the level of usage in these traditional areas has been steadily falling, despite such developments as the Irish language television station TG4, and the Irish language radio service RTÉ Raidió na Gaeltachta.

There are Gaeltacht areas in northwest Donegal and Tory Island; parts of west Mayo and the islands of Inishkea and Achill; Connemara in south Galway and the Aran Islands; the Dingle Peninsula in County Kerry; Muskerry and the island of Cape Clear in County Cork; An Rinn (the Ring) in Waterford and Ráth Cairn and Baile Ghib (Gibbstown) in Meath.

The Gaeltacht is the best place to listen to Irish and try out the phrases in this book, although you will meet Irish speakers everywhere, from the countryside to the cities. You may notice that there are differences in the Irish you hear from place to place. There are three distinct dialects: Ulster, Connacht and Munster, their names referring to the provinces in which they are largely spoken. Each dialect will have different ways of saying certain everyday phrases and some words will be different. Throughout this book you will find phrases from all dialects and we have used those forms which are most widely understood and easiest to use.

For more information on the Gaeltacht areas in Ireland and for information on holidays in the Gaeltacht, consult Gaelsaoire: www.gaelsaoire.ie.

GUIDE TO PRONUNCIATION

In this book, pronunciation of Irish words is given as a spelled-out representation based on English sounds. However, Irish is quite guttural (throaty sounds made with the soft palate), something which is not really found in English pronunciation, and so some of the representations are approximations, aiming to get as close to the sounds of Irish as possible, using pronunciation that is familiar to the reader.

For phonetic transcriptions of each word in IPA I recommend purchasing an Irish–English Dictionary. There are also several resources online where you can look up definitions and listen to pronunciations of Irish words. See www.focloir.ie and www.tearma.ie.

As a rule of thumb, 'ch' is pronounced as in the Scottish 'loch' or the German 'ch' sound. This is represented in this guide as 'kh'.

In some cases we use 'gh' to show that the sound is a little less guttural.

This is also the case quite often before the letter 't'. A further diminished 'h' is also used to differentiate another sound.

Do not be too worried about this, as any of these sounds apart from a '-ck' will most likely be understood.

A small number of sounds are impossible to illustrate correctly using English sounds but in those cases something very close has been substituted.

An important feature of Irish pronunciation is that consonants can be either 'broad' or 'slender' depending on the vowel next to them. Slender vowels are i and e. Broad vowels are a, o and u. Slender sounds are made with the tongue pushed up against the hard palate of the mouth, and broad sounds are made with the tongue pulled back towards the soft palate. Our pronunciation guide gives an approximation of these sounds, but the best way to learn about them is to hear them, and the websites www.focloir.ie and www.teanglann.ie have sound files that can help with that.

Emphasis on syllables is an area where you will notice a difference from north to south in Ireland. In the north the emphasis is usually on the first syllable, while in the south it is usually on the last syllable of any given word, except, in some cases, in very long words.

Hyphens have sometimes been used in the pronunciations in this book merely to break up sounds in words that are very long or that may be confusing to the eye. They are not an indication of how the word should be pronounced or of syllabic emphasis.

GETTING STARTED

Word order in Irish is often different from English. For example most sentences begin with the verb. Also, various expressions in English such as 'having' and 'wanting', amongst others, are expressed using prepositions:

I have money
Tá airgead agam   (Lit. 'money is at me')

There is no one word for 'yes' or 'no' in Irish, instead the verb in the question should be repeated in its affirmative (yes) or negative (no) form. Below are a few examples.

Will you have a drink?
An mbeidh deoch agat?
Un may jawkh ugut

Yes
Beidh
bay

No
Ní bheidh
Nee vay

16

Being understood

Would you like the bill?
Ar mhaith leat an bille?
Air wah lyat un bil-ye

Yes
Ba mhaith
Buh wah

No
Níor mhaith
Near wah

Being understood

I do not speak Irish
Níl Gaeilge agam
Nyeel Gayle-ga agum

I do not understand
Ní thuigim
Nee higgim

I am learning Irish
Tá mé ag foghlaim Gaeilge
Taw may egg fow-lim ayl-ge

Please repeat that slowly
Abair arís é go mall, le do thoil
Obber areesh ay guh mawl, leh duh hull

Can you help me?
An bhféadfá cuidiú liom?
Un vayd-faw cudge-oo lyum?

It does not matter
Is cuma
Iss cumma

I do not mind/ I don't care
Is cuma liom
Iss cumma lyum

17

Greetings and exchanges

Greetings and exchanges

Hello
Dia dhuit (to greet someone) / Dia 's Muire dhuit (in response to someone greeting you)
Dee-ah gwitch / Dee-ah smurra gwitch

Good morning
Dia dhuit ar maidin
Dee-ah gitch er modjin

Good night
Oíche mhaith agat
Ee-hah wah agut

Good-bye
Slán leat (to someone leaving your presence) / Slán agat (if you are leaving someone's presence)
Slawn lyat / Slawn agut

It is nice to meet you
Tá sé deas bualadh leat
Taw shay jass boola lyat

OK
Ceart go leor
K'yart guh lore

18

Greetings and exchanges

Please
Le do thoil
Leh duh hull

Thank you
Go raibh maith agat
Guh row mah agut

Excuse me
Go mo leithscéal
Guh muh leshkayle

Good
Go maith
Guh mah

I very sorry
Tá mé buartha
Taw may boor-ha

How are you?
Conas atá tú (Connacht) / Cén chaoi a bhfuil tú (Munster) / Cad é mar atá tú? (Ulster)
Kunass ataw too / Kayne kwee ah will too / Guh jay mar ata too

I am very well, thank you
Tá mé go maith, go raibh maith agat
Taw may guh mah, guh row mah agut

Greetings and exchanges

It is good to see you
Tá sé deas tú a fheiceáil
Taw shay jass too ah eckawl

There are five of us
Tá méid cúigéar ann
Taw-midge koogar unn

> **This is — my son**
> Seo é — mo mhac
> *Shoh ay — muh wak*

> **— my husband**
> Seo é — m'fhear céile
> *Shoh ay — muh arr kayla*

> **— my daughter**
> Seo í — m'iníon
> *Shoh ee — muh ineen*

> **— my wife**
> Seo í — mo bhean chéile
> *Shoh ee — muh van khayla*

My name is . . .
.... is ainm dom
.... iss annyim dum

Greetings and exchanges

What is your name?
Cad is ainm duit?
Kad iss annyim ditch?

I am a student
Is mac léinn mé
Iss mak lyayne may

I am on holiday
Tá mé ar saoire
Taw may er seera

I live in London
Tá cónaí orm i Londain
Taw koney urm ih Lunden

You are very kind
Tá tú an-chineálta
Taw too un-khin-yawlta

You're welcome!
Tá fáilte romhat
Taw fawl-cha rowat

See you soon
Feicfidh mé ar ball thú
Feckee may er ball hoo

I am from — America
Is as — Meiriceá mé
Is uss — Merikaw may

21

Greetings and exchanges

I am from — Australia
Is as — an Astráil mé
Is uss — un Ostrawl may

— Britain
Is as — an Bhreatain mé
Is uss — un Vratan may

— Canada
Is as — Ceanada mé
Is uss — Kyanada may

— England
Is as — Sasana mé
Is uss — Sassana may

— Ireland
Is as — Éirinn mé
Is uss — air-inn may

— New Zealand
Is as — an Nua-Shéalainn mé
Is uss — un noo-ah hayle-inn may

— Scotland
Is as — Albain mé
Is uss — Alben may

Common questions

I am from — South Africa
Is as — an Afraic Theas mé
Is uss — un africk hass may

— Wales
Is as — an Bhreatain Bheag mé
Is uss — un Vratan Vyug may

Common questions

Where?	**How?**
Cá	Conas
Kaw	*Kunass*
Where is/are . . .?	**How much?**
Cá bhfuil	Cá mhéad
Kaw will	*Ka vayd*
Where were you?	**Who?**
Cá raibh	Cé
Kaw row too	*Kay*
When?	**Why?**
Cén uair	Cén fáth
Kayne oo-ir	*Kayne faw*
What?	**Which?**
Cad é/ céard	Cé acu
kad ay / kerd	*Kay acoo*

23

Common questions

How long will it take?
Cá fhad a thógfaidh sé
Kaw hadd ah how-gee shay

What is the problem?
Cad é é an fhadhb
Kad ay un ibe

Do you know a good restaurant?
An bhfuil bialann mhaith ar eolas agat
Un will bee-ah-linn wah er ole-ass agut

Do you mind if I . . . ?
An miste leat má . . .
Un mish-cha lyat ma

What is wrong?
Cad é atá cearr
Kad-ay ataw kyarr

What time do you close?
Cén uair a dhúnann tú (*singular*) / sibh (*plural*)
Kayne oo-ir ah ghoo-nan too / shiv

Where can I buy a postcard?
Cá háit ar féidir liom cárta poist a cheannach
Kaw hawch air fayd-jir lyum karta pwisht ah khyannokh

Common questions

Where can I change money?
Cá háit ar féidir liom airgead a mhalartú
Kaw hawch air fayd-jir lyum arrigid ah wal-artoo

Where can I change traveller's cheques?
Cá háit ar féidir liom seiceanna taistil a bhriseadh?
Kaw hawch gur fayd-ir lyum sheckinna tash-chill ah vrishoo

Where can we sit down?
Cá háit ar féidir linn suí
Kaw hawch air fayd-jir lin see

Where is the toilet?
Cá bhfuil an leithreas
Kaw will un lyeh-riss

Who did this?
Cé a rinne seo
Kay ah rinn shoh

Who should I see about this?
Cén duine ar cheart dom labhairt le is faoi seo
Kayne dinna air khyart dum low-arch lesh fwee shoh

Will you come also?
An dtiocfaidh tú freisin
Un juc-ay too freshin

25

Asking the time

Asking the time

What time is it?
Cén t-am é?
Kayne tam ay

It is — nine-thirty pm (21:30)
Tá sé — leathuair tar éis a naoi san oíche
Taw shay — lah-oor tar aysh ah nee san ee-hah

— six-fifteen pm (18:15)
Tá sé — ceathrú tar éis a sé san oíche
Taw shay — kah-roo tar aysh ah shay san ee-hah

— a quarter past ten
Tá sé — ceathrú tar éis a deich
Taw shay — kah-roo tar aysh ah djeh

— a quarter to eleven
Tá sé — ceathrú chun a haon déag
Taw shay — kah-roo hun ah hayne-djayg

— after three o'clock
Tá sé — tar éis a trí a chlog
Taw shay — tar aysh ah tree ah khlug

— nearly five o'clock
Tá sé — beagnach a cúig a chlog
Taw shay — b'yugnokk ah koo-ig ah khlug

26

Asking the time

It is — twenty-five past ten
Tá sé — fiche a cúig tar éis a deich
Taw shay—fee-ha a koo-ig tar aysh ah djeh

— twenty-five to eleven
Tá sé — fiche a cúig chun a haon déag
Taw shay—fee-ha a koo-ig hun ah hayne-djayg

— eleven o'clock
Tá sé — a haon-déag a chlog
Taw shay—ah hayne-dayg ah khlug

— five past ten
Tá sé — a cúig tar éis a deich
Taw shay— a koo-ig tar aysh ah djeh

— half past ten
Tá sé — leathuair tar éis a deich
Taw shay— lah-oor tar aysh ah djeh

— five to eleven
Tá sé — cúig chun a haon déag
Taw shay— koo-ig - kun ah hayne-djayg

— ten o'clock
Tá sé — a deich a chlog
Taw shay— ah deh ah khlug

— ten past ten
Tá sé — deich tar éis a deich
Taw shay— djeh tar aysh ah djeh

27

Asking the time

It is — twenty past ten
Tá sé — fiche tar éis a deich
Taw shay—fee-ha tar aysh ah djeh

— twenty to eleven
Tá sé — fiche chun a haon déag
Taw shay—fee-hha hun ah hayne-djayg

— early
Tá sé — luath
Taw shay — loo-ah

— late
Tá sé — mall
Taw shay— mawl

— one o'clock
Tá sé — a haon a chlog
Taw shay— ah hayne ah khlug

— around midday
Tá sé — timpeall meán lae
Taw shay— chimp-all man-lay

— around midnight
Tá sé — timpeall meán oíche
Taw shay— chimp-all man ee-hah

28

Asking the time

at about one o'clock
timpeall a haon a chlog
chimp-all ah hayne ah khlug

at half past six
ag leathuair tar éis a sé
egg lah-oor tar aysh ah shay

at half past eight exactly
díreach ag leathuair tar éis a hocht
djeerakh egg lah-oor tar aysh ah hokht

in an hour's time
i gceann uaire
ih gyown oora

this morning
ar maidin
air modjin

in half an hour
i gceann leathuaire
ih gyown lah-oor-ih

tonight
anocht
an-okht

soon
go luath
guh loo-ah

two hours ago
dhá uair ó shin
ghaw oor oh hinn

this afternoon
an tráthnóna seo
on traw-no-na shoh

at night
san oíche
san ee-ha

this evening
anocht
an-okht

29

Common problems

Common problems

I am late
Tá mé mall
Taw may mawl

I cannot find my driving licence
Ní féidir liom mo cheadúnas tiomána a fháil
Nee fayd-jir lyum muh khyadoonass t'yum-awna ah awl

I have dropped a contact lens
Thit lionsa tadhaill de mo chuid
Hitch l'yunsa tayell du mu khudge

I have lost — my credit cards
Chaill mé mo — chártaí creidmheasa
Khyle may muh — khortee kredge-vassa

— my key
Chaill mé mo — eochair
Kyle may muh — ukher

— my traveller's cheques
Chaill mé mo — sheiceanna taistil
Khyle may muh — heckinna tash-chill

I have no currency
Níl aon airgead agam
Nyeel ayne arrigid agum

30

Common problems

I must see a lawyer
Caithfidh mé labhairt le dlíodóir
Kohhey may low-irtch leh dlee-oh-door

My car has been stolen
Goideadh mo ghluaisteán
Gwidge-oo muh ghlooshtawn

My handbag has been stolen
Goideadh mo mhála láimhe
Gwidge-oo muh wawla lawva

My wallet has been stolen
Goideadh mo sparán
Gwidge-oo muh sparawn

Is it safe — to go there?
An bhfuil sé sábháilte — dul ann?
Un will shay saw-vawl-cheh — dull ann

— to walk here?
An bhfuil sé sábháilte — siúl anseo?
Un will shay saw-vawl-cheh — shoo-il unshoh

— late at night?
An bhfuil sé sábháilte — go mall san oíche?
Un will shay saw-vawl-cheh — guh mawl sun ee-hah

AT THE AIRPORT

Ireland is served by international airports at Dublin, Shannon, Cork and Belfast. There are also several regional airports. Therefore Ireland can be easily reached by air from all major cities in Europe and is particularly well-served by the airports of the British Isles.

Airlines flying regularly to Ireland include Aer Lingus, British Airways, British Midland and Ryanair, and a large number of cheap flights are available if travelling from the British Isles.

Dublin International Airport is located to the north of Dublin city on the M1 and M50 motorways. You can fly to Dublin Airport from most European airports, and from Dublin Airport you can travel by bus, car or taxi or connect to nearby Connolly or Heuston train stations. Shannon International Airport is located 15 miles north of Limerick city and 15 miles south of Ennis. It has daily flights to and from most UK airports and is accessible by bus and car and has connections to nearby train stations. Cork Airport is located 4 miles south of Cork city.

Ireland West Airport Knock is the fourth busiest airport in Ireland after Dublin, Cork and Shannon, situated south of Charlestown and is the biggest airport serving the west/ northwest coast. It has daily flights to and from the UK.

Arrival

Here is my passport
Seo é mo phas
Shoh ay muh fas

How long will this take?
Cá fhad a thógfaidh seo?
Caw hadd ah howgee shoh

I am attending a convention
Tá mé ag freastal ar choinbhinsiún
Taw may egg frasstal er khonvinshoon

I am here on business
Tá mé anseo chun plé le cúrsaí gnó
Taw may unshoh hun play leh koorsee gnow

I will be staying here for eight weeks
Beidh mé ag fanacht anseo ar feadh ocht seachtaine
Bay may egg fanokht unshoh er fah okht shokhtin-ye

We are visiting friends
Táimid ag tabhairt cuairte ar chairde
Taw-midge egg tow-arch kurtche er kharja

How much do I have to pay?
Cá mhéad atá orm a íoc
Kay vayd ataw urm a eek

33

Arrival

I have nothing to declare
Níl aon rud le hadmháil agam
Nyeel ayne rud leh hadwawl aggum

I have the usual allowances
Tá na gnáthliúntais agam
Taw nah gnawhh lyoontish uggum

It is for my own use
Is do mo úsáid féin atá sé
Iss duh muh oosawj fayne ataw shay

I have checked in online
Sheiceáil mé isteach ar-líne
Heck-awl may iss-chah er-leena

I have printed my boarding pass
Tá mo phas bordála priontáilte agam
Taw muh fas board-awla print-awl-cheh agum

Here is my e-ticket
Seo duit mo thicéad leictreonach
Shoh ditch muh hickayd lyek-trone-uch

I paid for extra legroom
D'íoc mé as spás breise do na cosa
Deek may as spaws bresha duh na kusah

34

Common problems and requests

Can I upgrade to first class?
An féidir liom uasghrádú go dtí an chéad ghrád?
Un fayd-ijr lyum oo-as-grad-oo guh djee un khayd ghrawde?

I have lost my ticket
Chaill mé mo thicéad
Khyle may muh hickayd

I have missed my connection
Chaill mé mo eitilt fhreagrach
Kyle may muh etch-ilt rag-rok

Please give me back my passport
Tabhair mo phas ar ais dom le do thoil
Tow-ar muh fas er ash dum leh duh hull

The people who were to meet me have not arrived
Níor tháinig na daoine a bhí chun bualadh liom
Neer hawn-ig nah deenee ah vee hun boola lyum

Where can I find the airline representative?
Cá bhfuil ionadaí na haerlíne
Kaw will unadee na hairrlyeena

Luggage

Where do I get the connecting flight to Derry?
Cá bhfuil an eitilt fhreagrach go Doire
Kaw will un etch-ilt rag-rok guh-dirra

Where is — the bar?
Cá bhfuil — an beár
Kaw will — un barr

— the departure lounge?
Cá bhfuil — an seomra imeachta
Kaw will — un showmra imokhta

— the information desk?
Cá bhfuil — an deasc eolais
Kaw will — un desk ole-ish

— the transfer desk?
Cá bhfuil — an deasc aistrithe
Kaw will — un jask ashtriha

— the toilet?
Cá bhfuil — an leithreas
Kaw will — un lyehriss

Is there a bus into town?
An bhfuil bus ag dul go dtí an chathair?
Un will bus egg dull guh djee un khohher

How long will the delay be?
Cá fhad a mhairfidh an mhoill?
Kaw had a wirr-hee un will

36

Luggage

I was delayed at the airport
Cuireadh moill orm ag an aerfort
Cur-oo mwill orr-um egg un airfort

My flight was late
Cuireadh moill ar mo eitilt
Cur-oo mwill air muh etch-ilt

I was held up at immigration
Cuireadh moill orm ag an oifig inimirce
Cur-oo mwill orr-um egg un iffig inimirka

Luggage

Where is the baggage from flight number . . . ?
Cá bhfuil an bagáiste ó eitilt uimhir a . . .
Kaw will un bagawshta oh etch-ilt ivvir ah . . .

I have lost my bag
Chaill mé mo mhála
Khyle may muh wawla

These bags are not mine
Ní liomsa na málaí seo
Nee lyumsa nah mawlee shoh

Are there any baggage trolleys?
An bhfuil aon tralaithe bagáiste ann?
Un will ayne trawl-ee-ha bagawshta unn

37

Luggage

Can I have help with my bags?
An bhféadfainn cuidiú a fháil le mo chuid bagáiste?
Un vayd-finn cudge-oo ah awl le muh hidge bagawshta

Is there any charge?
An bhfuil aon chostas air?
Un will ayne khustas air

My baggage has not arrived yet
Níor tháinig mo chuid bagáiste go fóill
Neer hawn-ig muh hidge bagawshta guh foyle

Where is my bag?
Cá bhfuil mo mhála?
Kaw will muh wawla

It is — a large suitcase
  Is — mála taistil mór é
 Iss — mawla tashtil more ay

— a rucksack
  Is — mála droma é
 Iss — mawla drumma ay

— a small bag
  Is — mála beag é
 Iss — mawla b'yug ay

This package is fragile
Tá an beart seo sobhriste
Taw un bart shoh su-vrishta

AT THE HOTEL

Ireland has a great range of hotel accommodation from small, family-run establishments to five-star city and country hotels. Prices are generally per person rather than per room and breakfast is often included, but not always. It is advisable to check before booking.

The National Tourism Development Authority, known as Fáilte Ireland, regulates tourist accommodation in Ireland, and their organisation Discover Ireland can provide information on hotels and other accommodation.

A good guide to hotel quality is Fáilte Ireland approval. If a hotel is approved it will advertise this and display this. It should also be borne in mind that smoking is not permitted in hotels in the Republic of Ireland.

Websites:

> www.discoverireland.ie
> www.ireland.com
> www.visitdublin.com
> www.failteireland.ie
> www.meetinireland.com

Reservations and enquiries

I am sorry I am late
Tá brón orm as bheith mall
Taw brone urm ass vehh mawl

I have a reservation
Tá seomra curtha in áirithe agam
Taw showmra kurha in orr-ihha agum

I shall be staying until July 4th
Beidh mé ag fanacht go dtí an ceathrú lá de mhí Iúil
Beye may egg fonakht guh djee un kahroo law de vee ool

I want to stay for five nights
Ba mhaith liom fanacht ar feadh cúig oíche
Buh wah lyum fonakht er fah koo-ig ee-ha

Do you have a double room with a bath?
An bhfuil seomra dúbáilte le folcadán agaibh?
Un will showmra doobawlcha leh fulk-hadawn ugiv

Do you have a room with twin beds and a shower?
An bhfuil seomra le dhá leaba agus cithfholcadán agaibh?
Un will showmra leh gaw labba agus kih-ulkadawn agwiv

Do you have a single room?
An bhfuil seomra singil agaibh?
Un will showmra shingil agwiv

Reservations and enquiries

I need — a double room with a bed for a child
 Tá — seomra dúbáilte le leaba do pháiste – uaim
 *Taw — showmra doobawlcha leh labba daw fawsht-che
  – wem*

   — a room with a double bed
 Tá — seomra le leaba dhúbailte – uaim
 Taw — showmra leh labba ghoobawl-cha – wem

   — a room with twin beds and bath
 Tá — seomra le dhá leaba agus folcadán – uaim
 *Taw — showmra leh ghaw labba oggus fulk-hadawn –
  wem*

   — a single room
 Tá — seomra singil – uaim
 Taw — showmra shingil – wem

   — a single room with a shower or bath
 Tá — seomra singil le cithfholcadán nó folcadán – uaim
 *Taw — showmra shingil leh agus kih-ulkadawn no fulk-
  hadawn – wem*

   How much is — full board?
 Cá mhéad a chosnaíonn — bord iomlán?
 Kaw vayd ah khusnee-on— board umlawn

   — half-board?
 Cá mhéad a chosnaíonn — leathbhord?
 Kaw vayd ah khusnee-on— lyah-woard

41

Reservations and enquiries

How much is it per night?
Cá mhéad a chosnaíonn sé i gcóir na hoíche?
Kaw vayd ah khusnee-on shay ih gore na heeha

Does the price include room and breakfast?
An bhfuil an seomra agus an bricfeasta san áireamh?
Un will un showmra oggus un brikfawsta san orr-ivh

Does the price include room and all meals?
An bhfuil an seomra agus gach béile san áireamh?
Un will un showmra oggus gakh bayla san orr-ivh

Does the price include room and dinner?
An bhfuil an seomra agus an dinnéar san áireamh?
Un will un showmra oggus un dinnayre san orr-ivh

Can we have adjoining rooms?
An féidir linn seomraí taobh le chéile a fháil?
Un fay-djir linn showmree teeve le hayla a awl

Can my son sleep in our room?
An féidir le mo mhac codladh inár seomra?
Un fayd-ir leh muh wak kulla inore showmra

Do you take traveller's cheques?
An nglacann sibh seiceanna taistil?
Un nlokann shiv sheckinna tash-chill

Which floor is my room on?
Cén t-urlár ar a bhfuil mo sheomra?
Kayne turlar air ah will mo h'yowmra

Reservations and enquiries

Do you have a laundry service?
An bhfuil seirbhís níocháin agaibh?
Un will serveesh nee-okhawn agiv

Do you have a safe for valuables?
An bhfuil taisceadán agaibh do rudaí luachmhara?
Un will tashkadawn agiv duh ruddee look-wara

Do you have any newspapers?
An bhfuil aon nuachtáin agaibh?
Un will ayne nookht-ine agiv

Do you have a car park?
An bhfuil carrchlós agaibh?
Un will korrklowss agiv

Do you have a cot for my baby?
An bhfuil cliabhán agaibh do mo leanbh?
Un will klee-avawn agiv duh muh lyann-oo

Do you have satellite TV?
An bhfuil teilifís satailíte agaibh?
Un will tellifeesh satchileech agiv

What is the voltage here?
Cad é an voltas anseo?
Kad ay un vole-tass unshoh

Is there wifi in the room?
An bhfuil wifi sa seomra?
Un will wifi suh showmra

43

Reservations and enquiries

Is there wifi in the bar?
An bhfuil wifi sa bheár?
Un will wifi suh varr

What's your wifi password, please?
Céard é an pasfhocal don wifi le do thoil?
Kerd ay un pas-ukal dun wifi leh duh hull

Is there a computer I can use?
An bhfuil ríomhaire a bhféadfainn a úsáid?
Un will reevarreh a vayd-finn ah oosawje

Is there a computer I can use to send an e-mail?
An bhfuil ríomhaire a bhféadfainn a úsáid le ríomhphost a chur?
Un will reevarreh a vayd-finn ah oosawje leh reev-fost ah chur

Is there a computer I can use to check in for my flight online and print my boarding pass?
An bhfuil ríomhaire a bhféadfainn a úsáid le seiceáil isteach ar-líne don eitilt agam agus le mo phas bordála a phriontáil?
Un will reevarreh a vayd-finn ah oosawje leh sheck-awl iss-chah er-leena dun etch-ilt agum agus muh fas board-awla ah frint-awl

Is there — a hairdryer (here)?
An bhfuil — triomaitheoir gruaige anseo?
Un will — trum-eehore groo-ageh unshoh

Reservations and enquiries

Is there — a lift (here)?
An bhfuil — ardaitheoir anseo?
Un will — ordahore unshoh

— a minibar (here)?
An bhfuil — mionbheár anseo?
Un will — minvarr unshoh

— a swimming pool (here)?
An bhfuil — linn snámha anseo?
Un will — linn snawva unshoh

— a telephone (here)?
An bhfuil — teileafón anseo?
Un will — tellafone unshoh

— a television (here)?
An bhfuil — teilifís anseo?
Un will — tellafeesh unshoh

— a trouser press (here)?
An bhfuil — fáisceán bríste anseo?
Un will — fawshkawn breeshta unshoh

Do you have a room service menu?
An bhfuil liosta agaibh de na seirbhísí atá ar fáil sna
seomraí?
*Un will lista agiv deh na serveeshee ataw er fawl sna
showmree*

45

Reservations and enquiries

Can I smoke here?
An féidir liom caitheamh anseo?
Un fay-djir lyum kih-hiv unshoh

Is there a market in the town?
An bhfuil margadh sa bhaile?
Un will morreg-oo sa wollya

Is there a Chinese restaurant (here)?
An bhfuil bialann Shíneach anseo?
Un will bee-alinn Heenock unshoh

Is there an Indian restaurant (here)?
An bhfuil bialann Indiach anseo?
Un will bee-alinn Indee-okh unshoh

Is this a safe area?
An áit shábháilte í seo?
Un awch haw-wallcha ee shoh

Where is the socket for my electric razor?
Cá bhfuil an soicéad do mo rásúr leictreach?
Kaw will un sukayd duh muh rawsure lyektrokh

What time does the hotel close?
Cén uair a dhúnann an t-óstán?
Kayne oo-ir a ghoonann un toh-stawn

What time does the restaurant close?
Cén uair a dhúnann an bhialann?
Kayne oo-ir a goonann un vee-alinn

46

When does the bar open?
Cén uair a osclaíonn an beár?
Kayne oo-ir a usklee-on un varr

What time is — breakfast (available)?
Cén uair a bheidh — bricfeasta – ar fáil?
Kayne oo-ir a vaye — brikfawsta – air fawl

— dinner (available)?
Cén uair a bheidh — dinnéar – ar fáil?
Kayne oo-ir a vaye — dinnayre – er fawl

— lunch (available)?
Cén uair a bheidh — lón – ar fáil?
Kayne oo-ir a vaye — lone – er fawl

Is the tap water safe to drink?
An bhfuil sé sábháilte an t-uisce buacaire a ól?
Un will shay saw-vawl-cheh un tishka boo-karr-eh ah ole

Where can I get bottled water?
Cá háit a bhféadfainn uisce i mbuidéal a fháil?
Kaw hawch a vayd-finn ishka ah awl

Service

Can I charge this to my room?
An bhféadfainn an costas seo a chur ar tháille mo sheomra?
Un vayd-finn un kustas shoh ah khur er htawlya muh h'yowmra

47

Service

Can I dial direct from my room?
An bhféadfainn glaoch díreach a chur ó mo sheomra?
Un vayd-finn glayoch deerokh ah khur oh muh h'yowmra

Can I have a newspaper?
An bhféadfainn nuachtán a fháil?
Un vayd-finn nookhtawn ah awl

Can I have my wallet from the safe?
An bhféadfainn mo sparán a fháil ón taisceadán?
Un vayd-finn muh sparawn ah awl own tashkadawn

Can I have the bill please?
An bhféadfainn an bille a fháil le do thoil?
Un vayd-finn un bil-ye ah awl leh duh hull

Can I make a telephone call from here?
An bhféadfainn glaoch a chur ón áit seo?
Un vayd-finn glayoch ah khur own awch shoh

Can I send this by courier?
An bhféadfainn é seo a sheoladh le teachtaire?
Un vayd-finn ay shoh a h'yowla leh chakh-tereh

Can I use my credit card?
An bhféadfainn mo chárta creidmheasa a úsáid?
Un vayd-finn muh khorta credge-vassa ah oosawje

Can I use my personal computer here?
An bhféadfainn mo ríomhaire a úsáid anseo?
Un vayd-finn muh reevarreh ah oosawje unshoh

Can I use traveller's cheques?
An bhféadfainn seiceanna taistil a úsáid?
Un vayd-finn sheckinna tash-chill a oosawje

Can we have breakfast in our room, please?
An bhféadfaimis bricfeasta a fháil inár seomra le do thoil?
Un vayd-fameesh brikfawsta ah awl inore showmra leh duh hull

Can you recommend a good local restaurant?
An molfá bialann mhaith áitiúil dom?
Un mull-fah bee-alinn wah awchool dom

I want to stay an extra night
Ba mhaith liom fanacht ar feadh oíche bhreise
Buh wah lyum fonakht er fah eeha vresha

Do I have to change rooms?
An bhfuil orm aistriú go seomra eile?
Un will urm ashtroo guh showmra ella

I need an early morning call
An bhféadfá glaoch a chur orm go luath ar maidin?
Un vayd-faw glayoch a khur urm guh loo-ah er modgin

I need — a razor
Tá — rásúr – uaim
Taw — rawsure – wem

49

Service

I need — some soap
Tá — gallúnach – uaim
Taw — galloonoch – wem

— some toilet paper
Tá — páipéar leithris – uaim
Taw — pawpayre lehhrish – wem

— some towels
Tá — roinnt tuáille – uaim
Taw — rinnch too-awlya – wem

I need to charge these batteries
Ba mhaith liom na cadhnraí seo a luchtú
Buh wah lyum na kine-ree shoh ah lukhtoo

I want to press these clothes
Ba mhaith liom na héadaí seo a phreasáil
Buh wah lyum na haydee shoh a fressawle

Is there a trouser press I can use?
An bhfuil fáisceán bríste anseo a d'fhéadfainn a úsáid?
Un will fawshkawn breeshta unshoh a djayd-hinn a oosawje

Please fill the minibar
Líon an mionbheár le do thoil
Lee-on un min-var leh duh hull

Please leave the bags in the reception
Fág na málaí san Oifig Fháiltithe le do thoil
Fawg na mawlee san iffig awltihha leh duh hull

Service

Please turn the heating off
Múch an teas le do thoil
Mookh un chass leh duh hull

Please, wake me at 7 o'clock in the morning
Glaoigh orm ag a seacht a chlog ar maidin, le do thoil
Glay urm egg ah shokht ah khlug er modgin leh duh hull

Can I have — my key, please?
An bhféadfainn — mo eochair – a fháil le do thoil?
Un vayd-finn — muh ukher – a awl leh duh hull

— an ashtray, please?
An bhféadfainn — luaithreadán – a fháil le do thoil?
Un vayd-finn — loohradawn – a awl leh duh hull

— another blanket, please?
An bhféadfainn — blaincéad eile – a fháil le do thoil?
Un vayd-finn — blankayde ella – a awl leh duh hull

— another pillow, please?
An bhféadfainn — ceannadhairt eile – a fháil le do thoil?
Un vayd-finn — cyun-ayarch ella – a awl leh duh hull?

— some coat hangers, please?
An bhféadfainn — roinnt crochadán – a fháil le do thoil?
Un vayd-finn — rinnch krokhadawn – a awl leh duh hull

51

Problems

Can I have — some notepaper, please?
An bhféadfainn — páipéar scríbhneoireachta – a fháil le do thoil?
Un vayd-finn — pawpayre skreev-nyore-akhta – a awl leh duh hull

My room number is 22
Fiche a dó is ea uimhir mo sheomra
Fihha daw ish ah ivvir muh h'yowmra

Please can I leave a message?
An bhféadfainn teachtaireacht a fhágáil le do thoil?
Un vayd-finn chakhterakht ah awgawle leh duh hull

Problems

Where is the manager?
Cá bhfuil an bainisteoir?
Kaw will un banishtore

I cannot close the window
Ní féidir liom an fhuinneog a dhúnadh
Nee fay-djir lyum un innyoge ah ghoonah

I cannot open the window
Ní féidir liom an fhuinneog a oscailt
Nee fay-djir lyum un innyoge ah uskalch

Problems

The air conditioning is not working
Níl an t-aeroiriúnú ag obair
Nyeel un tayre-urroonoo egg ubber

The room key does not work
Níl eochair an tseomra ag obair
Nyeel ukker un chowmra egg ubber

The bathroom is dirty
Tá an seomra folctha salach
Taw un showmra fulk-ha sollach

The heating is not working
Níl an teas ag obair
Nyeel un chass egg ubber

The light is not working
Níl an solas ag obair
Nyeel un sulass egg ubber

The room is not serviced
Níl seirbhis déanta ar an seomra
Nyeel sherveesh djanta air an showmra

I can't get a mobile phone signal
Ní féidir liom comhartha fón póca a fháil
Nee fay-djir lyum coor-uh phone poke-ah ah awl

The room is too noisy
Tá an seomra seo róchallánach
Taw un showmra shoh row-khallanah

Checking out

There are no towels in the room
Níl aon túaille sa seomra
Nyeel ayne tooawlya sah showmra

There is no hot water
Níl aon uisce te anseo
Nyeel ayne ishka teh unshoh

There is no plug for the washbasin
Níl aon stopallán ann don bháisín níocháin
Nyeel ayne stuppalawn unn dun vawsheen nee-okhawn

Checking out

I have to leave tomorrow
Caithfidh mé imeacht amárach
Kohhee may imokht amore-okh

We will be leaving early tomorrow
Beidh muid ag imeacht go luath amárach?
Beye mwidge egg imokht guh loo-ah amore-okh

Could you order me a taxi?
An bhféadfá tacsaí a ordú dom?
Un vayd-faw taksay ah ordoo dum

Thank you, we enjoyed our stay
Go raibh maith agat, bhain muid taitneamh as ár gcuairt.
Guh row mah agut, win mwidge tatnev oss orr goorch

OTHER ACCOMMODATION

Other accommodation in Ireland includes hostels, bed and breakfasts, rented houses and camping and caravanning sites. Self-catering accommodation in Ireland can range from small apartments, to cottages, to renting a refurbished castle for your stay. Renting a house or cottage can be easily done through www.discoverireland.ie or in local tourist offices in the town in which you intend to stay. As with hotels and B & Bs, houses rented through tourist boards or on their recommendation will be guaranteed to conform to a certain quality.

> www.discoverireland.ie
> www.ireland.com
> www.visitdublin.com
> www.rent.ie/holiday-homes
> www.dreamireland.com

Renting a house

We have rented this house
Tá an teach seo faighte ar cíos againn
Taw un chokh shoh fye-cha er keess agwin

Renting a house

Here is our booking form
Seo é ár bhfoirm ordaithe
Shoh ay ore vwirrim orduhha

We need two sets of keys
Tá dhá fhoireann eochracha uainn
Taw ghaw irren ukhrackha wenn

Can I contact you on this number?
An bhféadfainn dul i dteagmháil leat ag an uimhir seo?
Un vayd-finn dull ih jagwall lat egg un ivvir shoh

Where is the bathroom?
Cá bhfuil an seomra folctha?
Kaw will un showmra fulk-ha

How does this work?
Conas a oibríonn seo?
Kunass ah ibree-onn shoh

I cannot open the shutters
Ní féidir liom na comhlaí fuinneoige a oscailt
Nee fay-djir lyum na kow-lee fwin-yowgih ah uskalch

Can you send a repairman?
An bhféadfá deisitheoir a chur chugainn?:
Un vayd-faw deshihore ah khur huginn

Is the water heater working?
An bhfuil an téiteoir uisce ag obair?
Un will un taychore ishka egg ubber

Do you have any spare bedding?
An bhfuil éadaí leapa breise agat?
Un will aydee lappa bresha agut

The cooker does not work
Níl an sorn ag obair
Nyeel un surn egg ubber

The refrigerator does not work
Níl an cuisneoir ag obair
Nyeel un kwishnore egg ubber

The toilet is blocked
Tá an leithreas blocáilte
Taw un lehriss block-aylcha

There is a water / gas leak
Tá éalú uisce / gáis ann
Taw ayloo ishka / gawsh unn

We do not have any water
Níl aon uisce againn
Nyeel ayne ishka agwin

When does the cleaner come?
Cén uair a thagann an glantóir?
Kayne oo-ir a hagann un glantore

Where is the fuse box?
Cá bhfuil an cóifrín fiúsanna?
Kaw will un kowfreen fyoosanna

57

Around the house

Where is the key for this door?
Cá bhfuil eochair an dorais seo?
Kaw will ukher an durish shoh

Around the house

bath	**cooker**
folcadán	sorn
Fulk-hadawn	*sorn*
bathroom	**corkscrew**
seomra folctha	corcscriú
showmra fulkha	*kork-shkroo*
bed	**cup**
leaba	cupán
lyabba	*cupawn*
brush	**fork**
scuab	forc
skoob	*fork*
can opener	**glass**
osclóir canna	gloine
usklore canna	*glinnya*
chair	**inventory**
cathaoir	liosta earraí
kohheer	*lista arree*

kitchen
cistin
kishtin

knife
scian
shkee-an

mirror
scáthán
skawhawn

pan
Panna
Panna

plate
pláta
plawta

refrigerator
cuisneoir
kwishnore

rubbish
bruscar
brooskar

sheet
braillín
brawleen

sink
doirteal
dorch-al

spoon
spunóg
spoonowge

stove
sorn
sorn

table
tábla
tabla

tap
sconna
skunna

toilet
leithreas
lehriss

Camping

vacuum cleaner (hoover)
folúsghlantóir
folooss-ghlontore

washbasin
báisín níocháin
bawsheen nee-okhawn

Camping

Camping in Ireland can be great fun and it is mostly restricted to campsites. The facilities on campsites can vary greatly, but most are very well equipped, with bathrooms, showers, cooking areas and playgrounds. Most campsites will have a store selling camping equipment such as bottled gas and other essentials. Some campsites will also have a restaurant or café. Many campsites will have large chalet tents or caravans to rent, so you may not even need to bring your own equipment. The full range of camping sites and their standards and facilities are described in a brochure available from the Irish Caravan and Camping Council.

Irish Caravan and Camping Council, Kilshanny,
Mitchelstown, Co. Cork
Email: info@camping-ireland.ie
Website: www.camping-ireland.ie

An app is also available from the website enabling you to search for campsites on your phone.

Camping rough

Camping rough is becoming rarer and rarer in Ireland, but it is allowed, with the landowner's permission.

Taking a caravan

Taking your own caravan to Ireland should not present any problems, however it is worth remembering that roads in rural areas can be very narrow. The Irish Caravan and Camping Council may offer certain discounts or special deals for visitors bringing a caravan to Ireland by ferry.

Caravans and speed limits:
Cars towing caravan/trailer not exceeding 750kg 100kph (62mph) on motorways; over 750kg 80kph (49mph) outside built up areas and 100kph (62mph) on motorways. If the total weight of the two vehicles exceeds 3,500kg, the limit outside built-up areas is 60kph (37mph) and 70kph (43mph) on motorways. To tow a caravan/trailer the weight of any caravan/trailer equipped with over-run brakes must not exceed the maximum weight of the towing vehicle.

Useful camping questions

Can we camp in your field?
An bhféadfaimis campáil i do pháirc?
Un vayd-fameesh kompaile ih duh fark?

Useful camping questions

Can we camp near here?
An bhféadfaimis campáil cóngarach don áit seo?
Un vayd-fameesh kompoil kongarakh dun awch shoh

Please can we pitch our tent here?
An bhféadfaimis ár bpuball a chur suas anseo le do thoil?
Un vayd-fameesh ore bubbell ah khur soo-ass unshoh leh duh hull

Can we park our caravan here?
An bhféadfaimis ár gcarbhán a pháirceáil anseo?
Un vayd-fameesh ore gorevawn a forkawl unshoh

Do I pay in advance?
An íocfaidh mé as roimh ré?
Un eek-ay may oss riv ray

Do I pay when I leave?
An íocfaidh mé as nuair a imím?
Un eek-ay may oss noor a imeem

Is there a more sheltered site anywhere?
An bhfuil láithreán níos foscúla áit ar bith?
Un will lawhrawn neess fuskoola awch er bihh

Is there a restaurant or a shop on the site?
An bhfuil bialann nó siopa ar an láithreán?
Un will bee-allin no shuppa er un lawhrawn

Useful camping questions

Is there another campsite near here?
An bhfuil láithreán campála eile in aice láimhe?
Un will lawhrawn kampawla ella in aykye live-a

Is this the drinking water?
An é seo an fíoruisce?
Un ay shoh un feerishka

The site is very wet and muddy
Tá an láithreán an-fhliuch agus lábach
Taw un lawhrawn un lyukh oggus labagh

Where are the toilets?
Cá bhfuil na leithris?
Kaw will na lehrish

Where can I buy gas?
Cá háit a bhféadfainn gás a cheannach?
Kaw hawch a vayd-finn gas ah khyannokh

Where can I have a shower?
Cá háit a bhféadfainn cith a thógáil?
Kaw hawch a vayd-finn kihh ah hoe-gile

Where can we wash our dishes?
Cá háit a bhféadfaimis na soithí a ní?
Kaw hawch a vayd-fameesh na soy-hee ah nee

Around the campsite

air mattress
tocht aeir
tukht ayir

backpack
mála droma
mawla drumma

bottle-opener
osclóir buidéil
usk-lore budjayle

bucket
buicéad
bukayde

camp bed
leaba champála
lyabba hompawla

camp chair
cathaoir champála
kohheer hompawla

can-opener
osclóir canna
usklore canna

candle
coinneal
kinyal

cup
cupán
kupawn

fire
tine
chinnya

flashlight
tóirse
torsha

fly sheet
leathán breise
lyaw-hun bresh-ya

folding table
tábla infhillte
tabla inillcha

fork
forc
fork

64

Around the campsite

frying pan
friochtán
frukhtawn

ground sheet
leahán talún
lyaw-houn taloon

ground
talamh
tolloo

guy line
téad
chaid

knife
scian
shkee-an

mallet
casúr beag
casoor by'ug

matches
cipíní
kipeenee

pail
buicéad
bukayde

penknife
scian phóca
shkee-ann fowka

plate
pláta
plawta

rucksack
mála droma
mawla drumma

shelter
dídean
djeejawn

sleeping bag
mála codlata
mawla kollata

spoon
spúnóg
spoonoge

stove
sorn
surn

tent peg
pionna pubaill
pyunna pubill

Hostelling

tent pole	**thermos flask**
cuaille pubaill	fleasc
koo-alye pubill	*flask*
tent	**torch**
puball	tóirse
pubble	*torsha*

Hostelling

There are many hostels in Ireland, offering good quality, affordable accommodation. The Irish youth hostelling association An Óige operates 22 youth hostels around the country. There are also six youth hostels in Hostelling International Northern Ireland. You must be an An Óige member or a member of the International Youth Hostel Association to stay in these hostels. There are also a great number of other quality hostels throughout the country. Most hostels will charge per bed, per night and accommodation is likely to be in dormitory rooms with shared bathroom and cooking facilities. Some hostels offer single, double or family or en suite rooms at higher rates, so it is worth finding this out before booking accommodation.

An Óige,
61 Mountjoy Street,   Email: info@anoige.ie
Dublin 7,   Phone: +353 (0)1 830 4555
Ireland.   Website: anoige.ie

Hostelling

Is there a youth hostel near here?
An bhfuil brú óige cóngarach don áit seo?
Un will broo oyga kongarakh dun awch shuh

Can we stay here five nights?
An bhféadfaimis fanacht anseo ar feadh cúig oíche?
Un vayd-fameesh fonokht unshoh er fah koo-ig eeha

Can we stay until Sunday?
An bhféadfaimis fanacht go dtí Dé Domhnaigh?
Un vayd-fameesh fonokht guh djee jay downee

Here is my membership card
Seo é mo chárta ballraíochta
Shoh ay muh khorta bollree-okhta

I do not have my card
Níl mo chárta agam
Nyeel muh khorta agum

Can I join here?
An bhféadfainn clárú mar bhall anseo?
Un vayd-finn klaroo mar wall unshoh

Are you open during the day?
An mbíonn sibh ar oscailt i rith an lae?
Un mee-an shiv er uskalch ih rih un lay

Can I use the kitchen?
An bhféadfainn an chistin a úsáid?
Un vayd-finn un khistin ah oosawje

67

Childcare

What time do you close?
Cén uair a dhúnann sibh?
Kayne oo-ir a ghoonann shiv

Do you serve meals?
An gcuireann sibh béilí ar fáil?
Un gwirrin shiv baylee er fawle

Can we get our meals to take away?
An bhféadfaimis ár mbéilí a thabhairt linn?
Un vayd-fameesh or maylee ah hoo-ert linn

Childcare

Can you warm this milk for me?
An bhféadfá an bainne seo a théamh dom?
Un vayd-faw un bonya shoh ah hayve dum

Do you have a baby chair?
An bhfuil cathaoir linbh agaibh?
Un will kohheer lyinn-iv agiv

Is there a baby-sitter (available)?
An bhfuil feighlí leanaí ar fáil?
Un will fye-lee lanee er fawle

Is there a cot for our baby (available)?
An bhfuil cliabhán ar fáil dár leanbh?
Un will klee-wawn er fawle dar lanniv

Is there a paddling pool (here)?
An bhfuil linn lapadaíola anseo?
Un will linn lapadeela unshoh

Is there a swimming pool (here)?
An bhfuil linn snámha anseo?
Un will linn snawa unshoh

Is there a swing park (here)?
An bhfuil páirc luascán anseo?
Un will park looskawn unshoh

I am very sorry. That was very naughty of him
Tá mé buartha. Bhí sé dána
Taw may boor-ha. Vee shay danna

It will not happen again
Ní tharlóidh sé arís
Nee harlowee shay areesh

How old is your daughter?
Cén aois í d'iníon?
Kayne eesh ee dineen

My daughter is 7 years old
Tá m'iníon seacht mbliana d'aois
Taw mineen shokht mleena deesh

My son is 10 years old
Tá mo mhac deich mbliana d'aois
Taw muh wok dehh mleena deesh

Childcare

She goes to bed at nine o'clock
Téann sí a luí ar a naoi
Tayann shee a lee air a nee

We will be back in two hours
Beidh muid ar ais i gceann dhá uair
Baye mwidge er ash i gyunne ghaw oore

Where can I buy some disposable nappies?
Cá háit a bhféadfainn clúidíní a cheannach?
Kaw hawch a vayd-finn cloo-jeenee ah khyannockh

Where can I change the baby?
Cá háit a bhféadfainn éadaí an linbh a athrú?
Kaw hawch a vayd-finn aydee un linve a ahhroo

Where can I feed my baby?
Cá háit a bhféadfainn mo leanbh a chothú
Kaw hawch a vayd-finn muh lanniv a khuhhoo

GETTING AROUND

Opening hours

Tourist offices generally open from 9am to 5pm, but in rural areas and small towns this can vary and some may operate a half-day or may close for an hour at lunch.

Similarly, post offices will generally be open from 9am to 5.30pm, but some country post offices may operate shorter hours. Rural post offices are unlikely to open at the weekend and all post offices will be closed on a Sunday.

Banks open from 10am to 4pm on Monday, Tuesday, Wednesday and Friday, with most banks opening until 5pm on a Thursday. Some banks in rural areas close for an hour at lunch. Very few banks will open at the weekend. Banks opening on a Saturday will be in city centres and will operate only limited services for a half-day.

Museums and archaeological attractions generally open from 9am to 5pm with guided tours available all day except for lunchtime. Most of these sites and all museums will be closed on Mondays.

Shops in cities and towns will open from 9am to 6pm and will often open until 9pm on Thursdays. Most large out-of-town shopping centres open from 9am until 6pm or 8pm on

Asking for directions

Saturdays, Sundays, Mondays and Tuesdays and from 9am to 9pm or 10pm on Wednesdays, Thursdays and Fridays. Some newsagents and convenience stores in towns and cities may stay open past midnight.

Asking for directions

Where is — the art gallery?
Cá bhfuil an — dánlann?
Kaw will un — dawnlonn

— the post office?
Cá bhfuil — oifig an phoist
Kaw will — iffig un fwisht

— the Tourist Information Service?
Cá bhfuil an — oifig eolais
Kaw will un — iffig ole-ish

Can you tell me the way to the bus station?
An bhféadfá insint dom cá bhfuil an busáras?
Un vayd-faw inshinnt dum caw will an buss-ore-ass

I am lost
Tá mé ar strae
Taw may er stray

72

Asking for directions

I am lost. How do I get to the Óstán na Rosann?
Tá mé ar strae. Cad é an bealach go dtí Óstán na Rosann?
Taw may er stray. Kad ay un bal-agh guh djee ostan na rosann

Can you show me on the map?
An bhféadfá é a thaispeáint dom ar an léarscáil?
Un vayd-faw ay ah hashpawnt doo er un lare-skawl

May I borrow your map?
An bhféadfainn do léarscáil a thógáil?
Un vayd-finn duh lare-skawl a howgawle

We are looking for a restaurant
Táimid ar lorg bialainne
Taw-midge ar log beea-linnye

Where are the toilets?
Cá bhfuil na leithris?
Kaw will na lehhrish

I am looking for the Tourist Information Office
Tá mé an Oifig Eolais ar lorg agam
Taw an iffig ole-ash ar lorg ugum

I am trying to get to the market
Tá mé ag iarraidh teacht ar an mhargadh
Taw may egg eerree chokht er un woruhga

Directions – by road

Can you walk there? (Can it be walked to?)
An bhféadfaí siúl ann?
Un vayd-fee shool unn

Is it far (from here)?
An bhfuil sé i bhfad ón áit seo?
Un will shay ih wodd own awch shoh

I want to go to the theatre
Tá mé ag iarraidh dul chuig an amharclann
Taw may egg eerree dull hig un owerklonn

Is there a bus that goes there?
An dtéann bus ansin?
Un djayonn bus unshin

Where do I get a bus for the city centre?
Cá bhfaighidh mé bus go lár na cathrach?
Kaw wee-ay may bus guh lawr na kohrokh

Is there a train that goes there?
An dtéann traein ansin?
Un djayonn trayne unshin

Directions – by road

Where does this road go to?
Cá dtéann an bóthar seo?
Kaw djayonn un bowhar shuh

74

Directions – by road

Do I turn here for Belfast?
An gcasaim anseo faoi choinne Bhéal Feirste?
Un gossum unshoh fah khonnye vale fresh-tcha

How do I get onto the motorway?
Conas a rachaidh mé ar an mhótarbhealach?
Kunass a ra-hay may er un wotarvallokh

How far is it to Galway?
Cá fhad atá sé go Gaillimh?
Kaw had ataw shay guh gall-yiv

How long will it take to get there?
Cá fhad a thógfaidh sé dul ann?
Caw had a hogey shay dull unn

I am looking for the next exit
Tá an chéad bhealach amach eile á lorg agam
Taw un khayd vallokh amoh ella aw lurg uggum

Is there a filling station near here?
An bhfuil aon stáisiún peitril cóngarach don áit seo?
Un will ayne stawshoon petchril kongarakh dun awtch shuh

Is this the right way to the supermarket?
An é seo an treo ceart go dtí an t-ollmhargadh?
Un ay shoh un trow k'yart guh djee un tollworuhga

Which is the best route to Derry?
Cad é an bealach is fearr go Doire?
Kadj ay un bal-agh iss f'yarr guh dirra

Directions

Which is the fastest route?
Cad é an bealach is gasta?
Kad ay an bal-agh iss gasta

Which road do I take to Cork?
Cen bóthar ba cheart dom a thógáil go Corcaigh?
Kayne bowhar buh kh'yart dom a howgawle guh cor-kee

Directions

You go — as far as . . .
Téann tú — chomh fada le . . .
Chayonn too — khow fodda leh . . .

— left
Téann tú — ar clé
Tayonn too — er klee

— right
Téann tú — ar dheis
Tayonn too — er yesh

You go towards . . .
Téann tú i dtreo . . .
Tayonn too ih djraw . . .

It is — at the crossroads
Tá sé — ag an gcrosbhóthar
Taw shay — egg un grusswo-har

76

It is — around the corner
Tá sé — timpeall an chúinne
Taw shay — chimpell un khoonya

— under the bridge
Tá sé — faoin droichead
Taw shay — fween drihed

— after the traffic lights
Tá sé — i ndiaidh na soilse tráchta
Taw shay — ih nyay na sulsha trawkhta

— next to the cinema
Tá sé — in aice na pictiúrlainne
Taw shay — in ekke na pick-chure-linnya

— on the next floor
Tá sé — ar an chéad urlár eile
Taw shay — er un khyayd ur-lawr ella

— opposite the railway station
Tá sé — os comhair an stáisiúin traenach
Taw shay — ose kowwer an stawshooin traynagh

— over there
Tá sé — thall ansin
Taw shay — holl unshin

Cross the street
Trasnaigh an bóthar
Trassnee un bowhar

Directions – what you may hear

Follow the signs for . . .
Lean na comharthaí do . . .
Lyan na ko-ar-hee doh . . .

> **Follow the signs for — the next junction**
> Lean na comharthaí — don chéad ghabhal eile
> *Lyan na ko-arr-hee — dun kh'ayd ghaw-wall ella*

> **— the motorway**
> Lean na comharthaí — don mhótarbhealeach
> *Lyan na ko-arr-hee — dun wotarvallagh*

> **— the square**
> Lean na comharthaí — don chearnóg
> *Lyan na ko-arr-hee — dun khyarnoge*

Keep going straight ahead
Gabh díreach ar aghaidh
Go djeeragh air ay

Turn left
Cas ar clé
Koss er klay

Turn right
Cas ar dheis
Koss er yesh

You have to go back
Tá ort dul ar ais
Taw urt dull er ash

78

Take the first road on the right
Tóg an chéad bhóthar ar dheis
Towg un khyayd wihear er yesh

Take the road for Limerick
Tóg an bóthar go Luimneach
Towg un bohar guh lim-ragh

Take the second road on the left
Tóg an dara bóthar ar clé
Towg un darra bohar er klay

Hiring a car

There are many different car rental companies operating in
Ireland so renting a car should not be a problem as long as
you have an International Drivers' Permit or an EU driving
licence. Different car rental companies will have their own
policies regarding age limits and insurance, so it is best to
shop around. It is worth remembering that renting a car at
an airport is likely to be more expensive. Also many rent-a-
car companies will have offices in Britain for you to arrange
your rental in advance.

I want to hire a car
Ba mhaith liom gluaisteán a fháil ar cíos
Buh wah lyum glooshtawn ah awl er keess

79

Hiring a car

I need it for two weeks
Beidh sé uaim ar feadh coicíse
Beye shay woo-im er fah kokeesha

Can I hire a car?
An bhféadfainn gluaisteán a fháil ar cíos
Un vayd-finn glooshtawn ah awl er keess

Can I hire a car with an automatic gearbox?
An bhféadfainn gluaisteán a fháil ar cíos le giarbhosca
uathoibríoch
*Un vayd-hinn glooshtawn ah awl er keess leh geervuksa
oo-ibree-agh*

Please explain the documents
Mínigh na cáipéisí, le do thoil
Meenee na kawpayshee leh duh hull

We will both be driving
Beidh an bheirt againn ag tiomáint
Baye un verch ag-inn egg chumawnch

Do you have — a large car?
    An bhfuil — gluaisteán mór agaibh?
      Un will — glooshtawn more ugiv

Hiring a car

Do you have — a smaller car?
An bhfuil — gluaisteán níos lú agaibh?
Un will — glooshtawn neess loo ugiv

— an automatic?
An bhfuil — gluaisteán uathoibríoch agaibh?
Un will — glooshtawn oo-ibree-agh agiv

— a diesel car?
An bhfuil — gluaisteán díosail agaibh?
Un will — glooshtawn jee-sil agiv

I would like to leave the car at the airport
Ba mhaith liom an gluaisteán a fhágáil ag an aerfort
Buh wah lyum un glooshtawn a awgawl egg un ayrefort

Is there a charge per mile?
An bhfuil an costas in aghaidh gach míle?
Un will un kustas in ay gagh meela

Must I return the car here?
An bhfuil orm an gluaisteán a thabhairt ar ais anseo?
Un will urm un glooshtawn a how-erch er ash unshoh

Can I pay for insurance?
An bhféadfainn íoc as árachas
Un vayd-finn eek oss awrahass

81

Hiring a car

Do I have to pay a deposit?
An bhfuil orm éarlais a chur sa ghluaisteán
Un will urm ayrlish ah khur sa ghlooshtawn

How does the steering lock work?
Conas a oibríonn an glas stiúrtha?
Kunass ah ibree-onn un gloss st-yurha

I would like a spare set of keys
Ba mhaith liom foireann eochracha bhreise
Buh wah lyum fwirren ukhrackha vresha

Where is reverse gear?
Cá bhfuil an giar cúlaithe?
Kaw will un geer kool-ee

Where is the tool kit?
Cá bhfuil an bosca uirlisí
Kaw will un buksa urlishee

Please show me how to operate the lights
Taispeáin dom conas a oibríonn na soilse, le do thoil
Tashpawn dum kunass ah ibree-onn na sulsha leh duh hull

Please show me how to operate the windscreen wipers
Taispeáin dom conas a oibríonn na cuimilteoirí gaothscátha
*Tashpawn dum kunass ah ibree-onn na kimilchoree
gweeskawha*

By taxi

Taxis are easy enough to come by in towns and cities. There you will find that there are two different types of taxi. A taxi which has a roof sign can be hailed on the street or ordered to pick you up by phone. They charge on a meter system so you cannot agree a price in advance but if you ask the driver he should be able to give you an approximation. Hackney cabs have no roof sign, having a small yellow plate beside their registration plate. Hackneys cannot be hailed on the street but can by ordered to pick up by phone. Hackneys do not operate on a meter so you can agree a price in advance.

Where can I get a taxi?
Cá háit a bhféadfainn tacsaí a fháil?
Kaw hawtch a vayd-finn taksee a awl

Take me to the airport, please
Go dtí an t-aerfort, le do thoil
Guh djee un tayrefort leh duh hull

The bus station, please
An stáisiún bus, le do thoil
Un stawshoon buss leh duh hull

Please show us around the town
Tabhair ar cuairt muid timpeall na cathrach, le do thoil
Tow-ar koo-irtch midge chimpell na kohrakh leh duh hull

By taxi

Please take me to this address
Chuig an seoladh seo le do thoil
Hig un showlah seo leh duh hull

Could you put the bags in the boot, please?
An bhféadfá na málaí a chur sa chófra bagáiste, le do thoil
*Un vayd-faw na mawlee a khur sah khowfrah bagawshta
leh duh hull*

Turn left, please
Cas ar clé, le do thoil
Koss er klay leh duh hull

Turn right, please
Cas ar dheis, le do thoil
Koss er yesh leh duh hull

Wait for me please
Fan liom, le do thoil
Fon lyum leh duh hull

Can you come back in one hour?
An bhféadfá teacht ar ais i gceann uaire
Un vayd-faw chokht air ash i gyunne oora

Please wait here for a few minutes
Fan anseo ar feadh cúpla nóiméad, le do thoil
Fon unshoh er fah koopla nowmayje leh duh hull

By taxi

Please, stop at the corner
Stop ag an gcúinne, le do thoil
Stup egg un goonya leh duh hull

Please, wait here
Fan anseo, le do thoil
Fon unshoh leh duh hull

I am in a hurry
Tá deifir orm
Taw djeffir urm

Please hurry, I am late
Déan deifir le do thoil, tá mé mall
Djann djeffir leh duh hull, taw may mawl

How much is it per mile?
Cá mhéad a chosnaíonn sé in aghaidh gach míle
Kaw vayd a khusnee-on shay in aye gukh meela

How much is that, please?
Cá mhéad ar fad, le do thoil
Kay vayd air fad leh duh hull

Keep the change
Coinnigh an briseadh
Kunn-yee un brish-oo

By bus

Each major city has its own city bus service. Dublin's bus service is run by Dublin Bus, a national transport company, though some routes have been adopted by private bus companies. The bus services in the other cities are run by Bus Éireann, a different arm of the national transport company, Córas Iompair Éireann (CIE). These buses operate comprehensive routes and are generally frequent and punctual. Bus Éireann also operates services between cities and to most towns throughout Ireland. It is worth noting that certain route, particularly those to popular tourist destinations are also served by private bus companies. It is always worth shopping around as some private companies can offer cheaper prices and more direct routes. Presenting a student card will get you a sizeable discount on Bus Éireann bus services and on most private buses also. Smoking is banned on all buses.

Does this bus go to the castle?
An dtéann an bus seo chuig an caisleán?
Un djayonn un bus shoh hig un kashlawn

How frequent is the service?
Cé chomh minic is atá an tseirbhís?
Kay khow minnick iss ataw un cherveesh

By train

What is the fare to the city centre?
Céard é an costas chuig lár na cathrach?
Kerd ay un kustass hig lawr na kohrokh

Where should I change?
Cá háit ar cheart dom aistriú?
Kaw hawtch gur k'yart dum ashtroo

Which bus do I take for the football stadium?
Cén bus ba cheart dom a thógáil don staid peile
Kayne bus buh kh'yart dum towgawle dun stadge pella

Where do I get the bus for the airport?
Cá háit a bhfaighidh mé bus go dtí an t-aerfort?
Kaw hawtch wee-ay may bus guh djee un tayrefort

Will you tell me when to get off the bus?
An inseoidh tú dom cathain is ceart dom tuirlingt den bhus?
Un inshowee too dum kohhen is k'yart dum turlyinch den vus

When is the last bus?
Cathain a imíonn an bus deireanach?
Kohhen a im-ee-un un bus djerenokh

By train

All rail transport is controlled by Iarnród Éireann, another arm of the national transport company, CIE. Trains operate frequently between all of the cities and most towns along these routes will have a train station. Dublin also has a

By train

light rail system, known as the DART which runs along
the coast from Howth in north Dublin to Bray in county
Wicklow. Dublin also has a tram system with two lines. The
red line runs from Tallaght to the Point and from Saggart
to Connolly. The green line runs from Brides Glen to St
Stephen's Green through Sandyford. Smoking is banned
on all trains.

Can I buy a return ticket?
An bhféadfainn ticéad fillte a cheannach
Un vayd-finn tickayde fillcha a k'yannokh

A return (round-trip ticket) to Sligo, please
Ticéad fillte go Sligeach, le do thoil
Tickayde fillcha guh slig-ah leh duh hull

A return to Galway, first class
Ticéad fillte go Gaillimh, céad ghrád
tickayde fillcha guh gall-yiv, kayd ghrawd

A single (one-way ticket) to Omagh, please
Ticéad singil go dtí an Ómaigh, le do thoil
Tickayde shingle guh djee un ow-mee, leh duh hull

Second class. A window seat, please
Dara grád. Suíochán fuinneoige, le do thoil
Darra grawd. See-ukhawn fwinnyogeh, leh duh hull

Do I have time to go shopping?
An bhfuil agam dul a shiopadóireacht?
Un will am ugum dul a hupp-adore-aght

Can I take my bicycle?
An féidir liom mo rothar a thabhairt liom?
Un faydge-ur lyum muh ruhher a howe-ert lyum

Is this the platform for Bray?
An é seo an t-ardán go Bré
Un ay shoh un tordawn guh bray

What are the times of the trains to Dundalk?
Cad iad amanna na dtraenach go Dún Dealgan
Kod eed omonna na draynokh guh doon djalgan

How long do I have before my next train leaves?
Cé chomh fada is a thógfaidh sé sula n-imíonn mo chéad
traein eile?
*Kay khow fodda iss ah hogey shay sulla nimee-onn muh
khayd trayne ella*

Where can I buy a ticket?
Ca háit a bhféadfainn ticéad a cheannach?
Kaw hawtch a vayd-finn tickayde a k'yannokh

Where do I have to change?
Cá háit a mbeidh orm aistriú?
Kaw hawtch a may urm ashtroo

Where do I pick up my bags?
Cá háit a mbailím mo chuid málaí?
Kaw hawtch a malee-em muh khidge mawl-ee

By train

Can I check in my bags?
An bhféadfainn mo chuid mála a chur isteach?
Un vayd-finn muh kwidge mawla ah khur iss-chah

I want to leave these bags in the left-luggage
Ba mhaith liom na málaí seo a fhágáil i seomra an
bhagáiste
*Buh wah lyum na mawlee shoh ah awgawl ih showmra un
vagawshta*

How much is it per bag?
Céard é costas gach mála?
Kerd ay kustass gokh mawla

I shall pick them up this evening
Baileoidh mé iad um tráthnóna
Balyowee may eed um traw-noe-na

I want to book a seat on the intercity to Belfast
Ba mhaith liom suíochán a chur in áirithe ar an traein
idirchathrach go Béal Feirste
*Buh wah lyum see-ukhawn a khur in orr-ihha er un trayne
idjir-hohrokh guh Bail Fairsh-tche*

Is there — a lost property office?
An bhfuil — oifig earraí caillte ann?
Un will — iffig arr-ee cawl-che unn

By train

Is there — a buffet car (club car)?
An bhfuil — proinncharr ann?
Un will — prinn-khar unn

— a dining car?
An bhfuil — carráiste bialainne ann?
Un will — karawshta bee-allinna unn

— a restaurant on the train?
An bhfuil — bialann ar an traein?
Un will — bee-allinn er un trayne

Where is the departure board (listing)?
Cá bhfuil an clár traenach?
Kaw will un clawr train-agh

I lost my ticket
Chaill mé mo thicéad
Hile may mu hick-edd

What time is the last train?
Cén t-am a n-imíonn an traein deiridh?
Kayne tom ah nim-ee-on un trayne jerry

When is the next train to Derry?
Cathain a imíonn an chéad traein eile go Doire?
Kohhen a im-ee-on un khayd trayne ella guh dirra

When is the next train to Coleraine?
Cathain a imíon an chéad traein eile go Cúil Raithin?
Kohhen a im-ee-on un khayd trayne ella guh kolle rye-han

By train

Which platform do I go to?
Cén t-ardán a rachaidh mé ann?
Kayne tordawn a ra-hay may unn

Is this a through train?
An traein dhíreach í seo?
Un trayne yeerokh ee shoh

Is this the Newry train?
An é seo an traein go dtí an tIúr?
Un ay shoh un trayne guh djee unn chure

Do we stop at Drogheda?
An stopann muid ag Droichead Átha?
Un stupann mwidge egg droy-had ahhah.

What time do we get to Galway?
Cén t-am a sroichfimid Gaillimh?
Kayne tom ah sroy-hee mwidge gall-yiv

Are we at Bangor yet?
An bhfuilimid ag Beannchar go fóill?
Un will mwidge egg ban-khar guh fowle

Will we be there on time?
An mbeidh muid ann in am?
Un maye mwidge unn in om

Can you help me with my bags?
An bhféadfá cuidiú liom le mo chuid málaí?
Un vayd-faw kudg-oo lyum leh muh kwidge mawl-ee

92

By train

Is this seat taken?
An bhfuil éinne ina shuí anseo?
Un will ayne-ya inna shee unshoh

May I open the window?
An cuma leat má osclaím an fhuinneog?
Un kumma lyat ma usklee-em un inyoge

My wife has my ticket
Tá mo thicéad ag mo bhean
Taw muh hickayde egg muh van

Is my bag in the way?
An bhfuil mo mhála sa bhealach?
Un will an mawla sa valagh

You are not allowed to smoke here
Níl cead caithimh anseo
Nyeel k'yad kihe-hiv unshoh

This is my seat
Seo é mo shuíochán
Shoh ay muh hee-khawn

Where is the toilet?
Cá bhfuil an leithreas?
Kaw will un lehriss

Why have we stopped?
Cén fáth ar stop muid?
Kayne faw air stup mwidge

93

DRIVING

Driving can be one of the best ways to explore Ireland and you will find little difference between the experience of driving in Britain and that of driving in Ireland. As long as you are over 17, have a pink EU licence and a fully insured car you will be able to drive in Ireland.

The roads

Ireland has limited motorways, most roads are known as national roads or regional roads. An examples of road names are as follows: Motorway, M50; national road, N34; regional road, R112. National roads are usually of good quality and are often dual carriageways. Regional roads can vary and some country roads can be very small indeed. Most roads outside of cities and towns will not be lit by street lamps but will have either reflective posts at the sides or reflective 'cat's eyes' in the centre of the road.

The rules

The rules of the roads and the speed limits are similar to those in Great Britain. Speed limits are 30mph in built-up

Traffic and weather conditions

areas and on some country roads, 60mph on main roads and 70mph on motorways. All passengers must wear seat-belts in the front and rear of cars and children under 12 may not sit in the front passenger seat. Using a mobile phone while driving is strictly forbidden unless you use a hands-free device. Driving while over the alcohol limit is forbidden and will incur severe penalties.

Traffic and weather conditions

Are there any hold-ups?
An bhfuil bac ar an trácht?
Un will bok air un trawght

Is the traffic heavy?
An bhfuil an trácht trom?
Un will un trawkt trum

Is the traffic one-way?
An bhfuil trácht aontreo?
Un will trawkt ayne-trow unn

Is there a different way to the stadium?
An bhfuil aon slí eile chuig an staid?
Un will ayne shlee ella hig un shtad

Is there a toll on this motorway?
An bhfuil dola ar an mhótarbhealach seo?
Un will dulla air un wowtar-vallagh shoh

Traffic and weather conditions

What is causing this traffic jam?
Céard is cúis leis an bhrú tráchta seo?
Kerd iss kooshlesh un vroo trawkhta shoh

What is the speed limit?
Céard í an teorainn luais?
Kerd ee un chore-ann loo-ish

What time does the car park close?
Cén t-am a ndúnann an carrchlós?
Kayne tom a noonann un korr-khlose

When is the rush hour?
Cathain a bhíonn an tráth brúite ann?
Kohhen a vee-on un traw broo-cha unn

Do I need snow chains?
An bhfuil slabhraí sneachta uaim?
Un will slowree shnokta woo-im

Is the pass open?
An bhfuil an mám oscailte?
Un will un mawm uskalcha

Is the road to Gweedore snowed up?
An bhfuil an bóthar go Gaoth Dobhair druidte le sneachta?
Un will un bowhar guh Ghee Doe-urr drudta le shnokhta

When will the road be clear?
Cathain a bheidh an bóthar oscailte?
Kohhen a veye un bowhar shoh uskalcha

96

Parking

Most shopping centres and other public amenities will have free parking, but some car parks may charge a fee. Similarly, parking in towns and cities is usually on a pay and display basis and your parking disc or receipt from a parking meter must be clearly displayed inside your front windshield. Be careful to be on the lookout for signs which forbid parking as cars parked illegally may be clamped.

Can I park here?
An bhfuil cead agam páirceáil anseo?
Un will k'yad aggum parkawl unshoh

Do I need a parking disc?
An bhfuil diosca páirceála uaim?
Un will djiska parkawla woom

Where can I get a parking disc?
Cá háit a bhféadfainn diosca páirceála a fháil?
Kaw hawtch guh vayd-finn diska parkawla a awl

Where do I pay?
Cá háit a n-íocfaidh mé?
Kaw hawtch ny-eek-ay may

Where is there a car park (parking lot)?
Cá bhfuil an carrchlós?
Kaw will un korr-khlowss

At the service station

How long can I stay here?
Cá fhad is féidir fanacht anseo?
Kaw hodd iss faydge-ur fonokht unshoh

Do I need coins for the meter?
An bhfuil boinn uaim don mhéadar?
Un will binn woom dun vaydar

At the service station

Do you take credit cards?
An nglacann sibh cártaí creidmheasa?
Un n-lokann shiv kortee credge-vassa

Can you clean the windscreen?
An nglanfaidh tú an gaothscáth?
Un n-lon-hee too un gee-skaw

Fill the tank please
Líon an t-umar peitril, le do thoil
Leen un tummar petchril leh duh hull

25 litres of — unleaded petrol
Cúig líotar fichid de — pheitreal gan luaidhe
Koo-ig lee-otar fihhid deh — fetchril gon loo-ee

— diesel
Cúig líotar fichid de — dhíosal
Koo-ig lee-otar fihhid deh —yee-ozal

At the service station

I need some distilled water
Tá uisce driogtha uaim
Taw ishka drigg-ha woom

Check the tyre pressure, please
Seiceáil brú na mbonn, le do thoil
Sheckawl broo na munn leh duh hull

The pressure should be 2.3 at the front and 2.5 at the rear
Ba cheart go mbeadh an brú dó pointe a trí chun tosaigh
agus dó pointe a cúig ag an gcúl
*Buh kh'yart guh may-oo un broo dow puncha a chree kun
tussee aggus dow puncha a koo-ig egg un gool*

My car is electric. Where is the nearest charging point?
Tá carr leictreach agam. Cá bhfuil an t-ionad luchtúcháin
is cóngaraí?
*Taw korr lyektrokh agum. Kaw will an tunnad luch-too-
khoyne iss kowne-garr-ee*

Check — the oil
Seiceáil an — ola
Sheckawl on — ulla

— the water
Seiceáil an — t-uisce
Sheckawl on — tishka

Breakdowns and repairs

Can you give me a push?
An bhféadfá an gluaistéan a bhrú?
Un vayd-faw un glooshtawn a vroo

Can you give me a tow?
An bhféadfá an gluaistéan a tharraingt?
Un vayd-faw un glooshtawn a harringch

Can you send a recovery truck?
An bhféadfá trucail tógála a chur chugam?
Un vayd-faw truckle toge-alla a khur huggum

Can you take me to the nearest garage?
An bhféadfá mé a thabhairt chuig an garáiste is cóngaraí?
Un vayd-faw may a howe-ert hiig un garawshta iss kowne-garree

Is there a telephone nearby?
An bhfuil teileafón in aice láimhe?
Un will chellafone in ekke live-ah

Can you find out what the trouble is?
An bhféadfá fáil amach céard atá mícheart?
Un vayd-faw fawl amah kerd ataw meek'yart

Breakdowns and repairs

Can you give me a can of petrol, please?
An bhféadfá canna peitril a thabhairt dom, le do thoil?
Un vayd-faw kanna petchril a howe-ert dum leh duh hull

Can you repair a flat tyre?
An bhféadfá bonn ligthe a dheisiú?
Un vayd-faw bunn ligheh a yeshoo

Can you repair it for the time being?
An bhféadfá é a dheisiú go sealadach?
Un vayd-faw ay a yeshoo guh shalladokh

Can you replace the windscreen wiper blades?
An bhféadfá na cuimilteoirí gaothscátha a athchur?
Un vayd-faw na kimiltorree gwee-skawha a ahh-hur

My car has broken down
Chlis mo ghluaisteán
Hlish muh ghlooshtawn

My car will not start
Ní thosóidh mo ghluaisteán
Nee husowee muh ghlooshtawn

Can you fix my exhaust?
An féidir leat an sceithphíopa a dheisiú?
Un faydge-ar lyat an skyeh-feepa a yeshoo

Breakdowns and repairs

Do you have jump leads?
An bhfuil seolaí tosaithe agat?
Un will showlee tuseeha aggut

Do you have the spare parts?
An bhfuil na baill spártha agat?
Un will na bwill sporha aggut

I have a flat tyre
Tá bonn ligthe agam
Taw bunn ligg-ha aggum

I have blown a fuse
Shéid mé fiús.
Hedge may f'yoos

I have locked myself out of the car
Chuir mé an gluaistéan faoi ghlas agus mé taobh amuigh de.
Khur may un glooshtawn fwee ghloss aggus may tayve amwih deh

I have locked the ignition key inside the car
Chuir mé an eochair faoi ghlas istigh sa ghluaistéan
Khur may un yaw-her fwee ghloss ishtee sa looshtawn

I have run out of petrol
Níl aon pheitreal fágtha agam
Nyeel ayne fetchril fawga aggum

Breakdowns and repairs

I need a new exhaust
Tá sceithphíopa nua uaim
Taw skyeh-feepa noo-ah woom

I think there is a bad connection
Ceapaim go bhfuil cónasc dona ann
K'yapam guh will kownawsk dunna unn

Is there a mechanic here?
An bhfuil meicneoir anseo?
Un will meknore unshoh

The engine has broken down
Chlis an t-inneall
Hlish un tinnall

There is something wrong
Tá rud éigin mícheart
Taw rud aygin meekhyart

There is something wrong with the car
Tá rud éigin mícheart leis an ghluaisteán
Taw rud aygin meekhyart lesh un looshtawn

Will it take long to repair it?
An tógfaidh morán am é a dheisiú
Un towg-hee shay more-unn ama ay a yeshoo

Is it serious (bad)?
An bhfuil sé go dona?
Un will shay guh dunna

Accidents and the police

My windscreen has cracked
Tá mo ghaothscáth briste
Taw muh ghee-skaw brishta

The air-conditioning does not work
Níl an t-aer-oiriúnú ag obair
Nyeel un tayre-urroonoo egg ubber

The battery is flat
Tá an bataire marbh
Taw un batara marv

The engine is overheating
Tá an t-inneall róthe
Taw un chinnyall row-heh

The exhaust pipe has fallen off
Thit an sceithphíopa as
Hitch un skeh-feepa ass

There is a leak in the radiator
Tá poll sa radaitheoir
Taw pull sa raddee-hore

Accidents and the police

If you are involved in an accident on the road you should either swap insurance information and contact information with the other party involved. If you are involved in a

Accidents and the police

serious accident or if you are in disagreement with the other party involved in the accident you should call the police. In Ireland the police force is known as An Garda Síochána, so you police officers, cars and police stations will be marked Garda and you will hear them referred to as 'the Gardaí' (pronounced Gardee) or simply 'the guards'.

There has been an accident
Bhí timpiste ann
Vee timpishta unn

We must call an ambulance
Tá orainn fios a chur ar otharcharr
Taw urreenn fiss a khur er uhher-horr

We must call the police
Tá orainn fios a chur ar na gardaí
Taw urrann fiss a khur er nah gordee

What is your name and address?
Céard é d'ainm agus seoladh?
Kerd ay danyam oggus showla

You must not move
Níl cead agat imeacht
Nyell kyad uggat imokht

Do you want my passport?
An bhfuil mo phas uait?
Un will muh fass woo-it

Accidents and the police

He did not stop
Níor stop sé
Neer stup shay

He is a witness
Is finné é
Iss feenay ay

He overtook on a bend
Scoith sé gluaistéan ar uillin ar bhóthar
Skuhh shay glooshtawn er illin air wow-her

He ran into the back of my car
Bhuail sé cúl mo ghluaisteáin
Wool shay kool muh looshtawn

He stopped suddenly
Stop sé go tobann
Stup shay guh tubann

He was moving too fast
Bhí sé ag bogadh róthapa
Vee shay egg bugga rowhoppee

Here are my insurance documents
Seo iad mo cháipéisí árachais
Shoh eed muh hawpayshee ore-ahish

106

Accidents and the police

Here is my driving licence
Seo é mo cheadúnas tiomána
Shoh ay muh khyadoonass chimawna

I could not stop in time
Ní raibh mé in ann stopadh in am
Nee row may in unn stuppa in om

I did not see the bicycle
Ní fhaca mé an rothar
Nee okka may un ruhhar

I did not see the sign
Ní fhaca mé an comhartha
Nee okka may un coe-arha

I did not understand the sign
Níor thuig mé an comhartha
Neer higg may un coe-arha

I am very sorry. I am a visitor
Tá brón orm. Is cuairteoir mé
Taw brone urm. Iss koorchore may

I did not know about the speed limit
Ní raibh a fhios agam faoin teorainn luais
Nee row iss ugamm fween chore-ann loosh

107

Accidents and the police

How much is the fine?
Cá mhéad atá ar an bhfíneáil
Kaw vayd ataw er un veenawl

Can I pay at the police station?
An bhféadfainn íoc aisti ag stáisiún na ngardaí?
Un vayd-finn eek ashtee egg stawshoon na nordee

I have not had anything to drink
Ní raibh aon deoch agam
Nee row ayne jawkh aggum

I was only driving at 50 mph
Ní raibh mé ag tiomáint ach ag caoga míle san uair
Nee row may egg chim-awntch okh egg kayga meela san oor

I was overtaking
Bhí mé ag scoitheadh gluaisteáin
Vee may egg skuhha glooshtawn

I was parking
Bhí mé ag páirceáil
Vee may egg parkawl

My car has been towed away
Tarraingíodh mo ghluaistéan ar shiúl
Tarr-ing-ee-oo muh looshtawn air hyule

That car was too close
Bhí an gluaistéan sin ró-chóngarach
Vee un glooshtawn shin row-howne-garra

108

Accidents and the police

The brakes failed
Theip ar na coscáin
Hepp er na kuskawn

The car registration number (license number) was . . .
Ba é clár-uimhir an ghluaisteáin . . .
Buh ay klore-ivvir un looshtawn

The car skidded
Sciorr an gluaisteán
Sckirr un glooshtawn

The car swerved
D'fhiar an gluaistéan
Dear un glooshtawn

The car turned right without signalling
Chas an gluaistéan ar dheis gan é sin a chur in iúl
Koss un glooshtawn er yesh gon ay shin a hur in ool

The road was icy
Bhí sioc ar an bhóthar
Vee shuck air un woe-har

The tyre burst
Phléasc an bonn
Flaysk un bunn

Car parts

accelerator
luasaire
loosara

aerial
aeróg
ayr-owge

air filter
aerscagaire
ayr-skoggara

alternator
ailtéarnóir
alcharenore

antifreeze
frithreo
frihhraw

axle
aiseal
ashill

battery
bataire
batara

bonnet
boinéad
bun-yade

boot
cófra bagáiste
kowfra bagawshta

brake fluid
leacht coscán
lyaght kuskawn

brakes
coscáin
kuskawn

bulb
bolgán
bulgawne

bumper
tuairteoir
too-archore

carburettor
carbradóir
karbradore

child seat
suíochán páiste
see-hawn posh-tche

choke
tachtaire
tagh-tirra

clutch
crág
krawg

cylinder
sorcóir
surkore

disc brake
coscán diosca
kuskawn jiska

distributor
dáileoir
dile-yore

door
doras
durass

dynamo
dineamó
jin-ammoe

electrical system
an córas leictreach
un kore-ass lyekht-ragh

engine
inneall
innyall

exhaust system
córas sceite
kore-ass sketcha

fan belt
crios gaothráin
kriss gee-hrawn

foot pump
pumpa coise
pumpa kusha

fuse
fiús
fyoos

fuel pump
pumpa breosla
pumpa brawlsha

fuel gauge
tomhas breosla
toe-wass browshla

111

Car parts

gear box
giarbhosca
geerwuksa

horn
adharc
eye-ark

gear lever
giarluamhán
gear-loo-wan

hose
píobán
pee-bawn

generator
gineadóir
ginnyadore

ignition
adhaint
eye-inch

hammer
casúr
kassoor

ignition key
eochair adhainte
uhher eye-incha

hand brake
coscán láimhe
kuskawn lawva

indicator
táscaire
toskirra

hazard lights
soilse guaise
sul-sha goosha

jack
seac
shack

headlights
ceannsoilse
kyunn-sul-sha

lights
soilse
sul-sha

hood
cumhdach
koodock

lock
glas
gloss

oil
ola
ulla

oil filter
scagaire ola
skoggara ulla

oil pressure
brú ola
broo ulla

petrol
peitreal
petchril

points
pointí
pwinchee

pump
pumpa
pumpa

radiator
radaitheoir
raddee-hore

rear-view mirror
scáthán cúil
skohhawn koo-il

reflectors
frithchaiteoirí
frihh-hotchore-ee

reversing light
solas cúlaithe
sulass kool-ee

roof rack
raca bagáiste
rokka bagawshta

screwdriver
scriúire
skree-urra

seat
suíochán
see-hawn

seat belt
crios sábhála
kriss sawalla

shock absorber
maolaire buille
mweel-irra bwilla

silencer
ciúnadóir
kyoonadore

113

Car parts

socket set
foireann soicéad
fwirren sokayje

stoplight
stadsolas
stodsulass

spanner
castaire
kast-irra

sun roof
díon gréine
djee-on graynyeh

spare part
ball spártha
boll spore-ha

suspension
crochadh
kruhhoo

spark plug
spréachphlocóid
sprake-flukodje

tools
uirlisí
urlishee

speedometer
luasmhéadar
loo-as-vayder

towbar
barra tarraingthe
borra torringha

starter motor
mótar dúisithe
mowtar doosh-ihha

transmission
tarchur
tar-hur

steering
stiúradh
st'yoora

trunk
cófra bagáiste
kowfra bagawshta

steering wheel
roth stiúrtha
ruh st'yoorha

tyre
bonn
bunn

warning light
solas rabhaidh
sulass rowwee

windscreen wipers
cuimilteoirí gaothscátha
kwimilchoree gee-skawha

wheel
roth
ruhh

wrench
rinse
rinsha

windscreen
gaothscáth
gee-skaw

Road signs

Private road
Bóthar príobháideach
Boe-her pree-vaw-jah

Drive slowly
Go mall
Guh mawl

Give way
Géill slí
Gayle shlee

Diversion
Atreo
A-chraw

Centre (of city, town, etc)
An lár
Un lawre

One way
Bealach aontreo
Ballagh ayne-trow

Ice
Sioc
Shuck

Car park
Carrchlós
Koor-klowss

115

Road signs

No parking permitted
Cosc ar pháirceáil
Kusk er farkawl

Danger
Dáinséar / Contúirt
Dawnshare / Konturch

Roadworks
Oibreacha
Ibrakha

Beware
Aire
Arra

No through road
Bealach dúnta
Ballah doonta

No thoroughfare
Ná téitear anseo
Naw chay-tchar unshoh

Toll
Dola
Dulla

No entry
Ná téitear isteach
Naw taytar iss-chah

EATING OUT

Ireland has some great opportunities for eating out. You can eat well but inexpensively or you can sample dishes in Michelin-star winning restaurants. There is a great selection of restaurants. It is a good idea to have a look at the menu on the wall outside the restaurant before entering as eating out in Ireland can sometimes be expensive.

Expect to encounter restaurants specialising in the cuisines of many countries – Mexican, Chinese, Indian, Thai, French etc. – and also fusion restaurants which offer the best of all tastes. For inexpensive and hearty food try large pubs which will often have a good value carvery lunch or serve dinner with several different roasts each day. *The Irish Food Guide*, www.guides.ie, tasteofireland.com and goodfoodireland.ie are all worth a look to give you ideas.

Reservations

Should we reserve a table?
Ar chóir dúinn focal a chur ar bhord?
Air hore doo-inn fukal a khur er vord

Useful questions

Can I book a table for four at 8 o'clock?
An bhféadfainn focal a chur ar bhord do cheathrar ar a hocht a chlog?
Un vayd-finn fukal a khur er vord duh khahhrar air a hukht a khlug

Can we have a table for four?
An bhféadfaimis bord do cheathrar a fháil?
Un vayd-fameesh bord duh khahhrar a awl

I am a vegetarian
Is feoilséantóir mé
Iss f'yowle-shine-tore may

We would like a table — by the window
  Ba mhaith linn bord — in aice na fuinneoige
    Buh wah linn bord — in ay-kye na fwinyowgeh

— on the terrace
  Ba mhaith linn bord — ar an lochtán
    Buh wah linn bord — er un lukhtawn

Useful questions

Are vegetables included?
An bhfuil glasraí san áireamh?
Un will glossree san ire-iv

118

Useful questions

Do you have a local speciality?
An bhfuil bia de chuid na háite agaibh?
Un will bee-ahde hudge na hatch-eh agiv

Do you have a set menu?
An bhfuil biachlár socraithe agaibh?
Un will bee-akhlore sukrahha agiv

What do you recommend?
Cad a mholfá dom?
Kodd a vulfaw doo

What is the dish of the day?
Céard é béile an lae?
Kerd ay bayla un lay

What is the soup of the day?
Céard é anraith an lae?
Kerd ay onreeh un lay

What is this called?
Céard a thugtar air seo?
Kerd a hugtar er shoh

What is this dish like?
Conas atá an béile seo?
Kunass ataw un bayla shoh

Which wine do you recommend?
Cé acu fíon a mholfá dom?
Kay-accoo fee-on a vulfaw doo

Ordering your meal

How do I eat this?
Conas a n-itear seo?
Kunass a n-itchar shoh

Is the wine good?
An bhfuil an fíon go maith?
Un will un fee-on guh mah?

Is this cheese very strong?
An bhfuil blas na cáise seo an-láidir?
Un will bloss na kawsheh shoh un lawdjir

Is this good?
An bhfuil sé seo go deas?
Un will shay shoh guh jass

What is this?
Céard é seo?
Kerd ay shoh

What do you have that is gluten-free?
Céard atá agat gan ghlútan?
Kerd ataw agut gon ghluten

Ordering your meal

The menu, please
An biachlár, le do thoil
Un bee-akhlore leh duh hull

Ordering your meal

I will take the set menu
Beidh an biachlár socraithe agam
Beye un bee-akhlore sukrahha aggum

Can we start with soup?
An bhféadfaimis tosú leis an anraith?
Un vayd-fameesh tusoo lesh un onreeh

I like my steak— very rare
Is maith liom mo stéig— an-scothbhruite
Iss mah lyum muh styayg— un skuh-vritcha

— rare
Is maith liom mo stéig—scothbhruite
Iss mah lyum muh styayg— skuh-vritcha

— medium rare
Is maith liom mo stéig— a bheith measartha scothbhruite
Iss mah lyum muh styayg— mas-ar-ha skuh-vritcha

— well done
Is maith liom mo stéig— déanta go maith
Iss mah lyum muh styayg— a veh daynta guh mohh

Could we have some butter?
An bhféadfaimis giota ime a fháil?
Un vayd-fameesh gyitta ima a awl

I will have salad
Beidh sailéad agam
Beye sallade aggum

121

Ordering drinks

I will take that
Tógfaidh mé é sin
Towg-hee may ay shin

That is for me
Beidh sin agam
B ay shin aggum

Could we have some more bread, please?
An bhféadfaimis tuilleadh aráin a fháil, le do thoil?
Un vayd-fameesh tilla arawn a awl leh duh hull

Can I see the menu again, please?
An bhféadfainn an biachlár a fheicéail arís, le do thoil?
Un vayd-finn un bee-akhlore a eckawl areesh leh duh hull

Ordering drinks

The wine list, please
An liosta fíona, le do thoil
Un lista fee-ona leh duh hull

A bottle of house red wine, please
Buidéal fhíon dearg an tí le do thoil
Bujayle een jar-ig un chee leh duh hull

A glass of dry white wine, please
Gloine fíona ghil thirim, le do thoil
Glinnya fee-ona yill hirrim leh duh hull

Ordering drinks

Another bottle of red wine, please
Buidéal eile fíona dheirg, le do thoil
Bujayle ella fee-ona yerrig leh duh hull

Another glass, please
Gloine eile, le do thoil
Glinyna ella leh duh hull

Black coffee, please
Caife dubh, le do thoil
Kafay doo leh duh hull

Can we have some (still / sparkling) mineral water?
An bhféadfaimis uisce mianra (gan ghás/coipeach) a fháil?
Un vayd-fameesh ishka meenra (gan ghoss / kuphoh) a awl

Coffee with milk, please
Caife le bainne, le do thoil
Kafay leh bonnya leh duh hull

Some plain water, please
Gnáthuisce, le do thoil
Graw-ishka leh duh hull

Two beers, please
Dhá bheoir, le do thoil
Gaw vyore leh duh hull

Can I have an alcohol-free beer?
An bhféadfainn beoir gan alcól a bheith agam?
Un vayd-finn b'yore gun al-cole ah vehh agum?

123

Paying the bill

Can we have the bill, please?
An bhféadfaimis an bille a fháil, le do thoil?
Un vayd-fameesh un billya a awl leh duh hull

Is service included?
An bhfuil an tseirbhís san áireamh?
Un will un cherveesh san ire-iv

Is tax included?
An bhfuil cáin san áireamh?
Un will kawn san ire-iv

Is there any extra charge?
An bhfuil aon chostas breise?
Un will ayne khustas bresha

I haven't enough money
Níl go leor airgid agam
Nyeel guh lyore argidge aggum

This is not correct
Níl sé seo ceart
Nyeel shay shoh k'yart

This is not my bill
Ní hé seo mo bhille
Nee hay shoh muh vill-ya

124

Complaints and compliments

You have given me the wrong change
Thug tú an briseadh mícheart dom
Hug too un vrish-oo mee-kh'yart doo

Complaints and compliments

This is cold
Tá sé seo fuar
Taw shay shoh foor

This is not what I ordered
Ní hé seo an rud a d'ordaigh mé
Nee hay shoh un rud a dorday may

Waiter! We have been waiting for a long time
A fhreastalaí! Tá muid ag fanacht le tamall fada
A rastalee! Taw midge egg fonokht leh tomall fodda

Can I have the recipe?
An bhféadfainn an t-oideas a fháil?
Un vayd-finn un tidgas a awl

The meal was excellent
Bhí an béile ar fheabhas
Vee un bayla air owwass

This is excellent
Tá sé seo ar fheabhas
Taw shay shoh air owwass

125

Food

Ireland has a diverse range of foods on offer. Many dishes and specialities will be similar to British ones, but make sure you sample the many breads, cheeses and alcoholic beverages which are particular to this part of the world: brown breads, soda breads, mature cheddars such as Dubliner, blue cheeses such as Cashel Blue and cottage cheeses such as Boilie. You will find the Irish take on food both familiar and unique.

Regional specialities

Many dishes are particular to Ireland or favoured by people in certain places. Make sure to sample the seafood along the west coast. Many counties are famed for their seafood chowder which can be thick and creamy like a soup or light like a consommé, but always excellent. Galway's Oyster Festival, usually held in September, will give you a chance to try Irish oysters, best served with Guinness stout.

The most famous of Irish dishes is the Irish Stew: a thick and filling stew of potatoes, carrots, onions and lamb. Irish stew can be flavoured with herbs and is a great dish for a cold day! Other stew-like dishes include Beef with Guinness, and Coddle (a dish consisting of bacon rashers, sausages, potatoes and onions, boiled like a stew). Some variations of Coddle include Dublin Coddle, in which the ingredients are cooked in cider.

Menu reader

apples
úlla
oolla

apple compote
'compote' úill
compote oo-ill

apple tart
úllchíste
oo-ill-kheeshta

apricots
aibreoga
aybrowga

asparagus
lus súch
looss sook

avocado
avocado
avocado

baked beans
pónairí bácáilte
pownaree bakawlcha

banana
banana
banana

basil
lus mic rí
luss mick ree

bayleaf
labhras
lowras

beef broth
anraith mairteola
unraih marchowla

beefburger
burgair
burgar

beefsteak
stéig mairteola
stayg more-chowla

black pudding (= sausage)
putóg dhubh
putowg ghooh

127

Menu reader

blackcurrants
cuiríní dubha
kwireenee duvva

braised beef
mairteoil ghalstofa
marchowl ghallstuffa

bread rolls
rollóga aráin
rullowga arawn

broad beans
pónairí leathan
pownaree lahhan

broth
anraith / brat
unraih / brot

Brussels sprouts
bachlóga Bhruiséile
baklowga vrushayla

butter
im
im

cabbage
cabáiste
kabawshta

Caesar salad
sailéad ceasar
shallayje caesar

cauliflower
cóilís
kowleesh

celery
soilire
shullarra

champ (mashed potatoes with scallions)
brúitín
brootcheen

cheese omelette
uibheagán cáis
ivvehgawn kawsh

cheese
cáis
kawsh

cherries
silín / silíní (pl.)
shilleen / shilleenee

chervil
camán gall
kamawn goll

chicken broth
anraith sicín
unraih shikeen

chicken pie
císte sícín
keeshta shickeen

chicory
siocaire
shickorra

chives
síobhás / síobháis (pl.)
Shee-ovaws / Shee-ovawsh

chocolate mousse
'mousse' seacláide
mousse shacklawdja

clams
breallaigh
brallee

colcannon
cál ceannann
colcannon

courgette
courgette
courgette

cucumber
cúcamar
kookamar

cured ham
liamhás saillithe
lee-awawsh sawlihha

dates
dátaí
dawtee

eggs with bacon
uibheacha le bagún
ivaka le bawgoon

129

Menu reader

eggs with ham
uibheacha le liamhás
ivaka le lee-awawsh

fillet steak
stéig filléid
stayg fillayje

fish
iasc
eeask

French fries (chips)
sceallógaí
shkallowgee

fried eggs
uibheacha friochtha
ivaka frukha

fried/breaded chicken
sicín friochta / le harán
shickeen frikhta / leh harawn

fritters
friochtóg / friochtóga (pl.)
frightowg / frightowga

fruit salad
sailéad torthaí
shallayje torhee

fruit with whipped cream
torthaí le uachtar coipthe
torhee leh ooktar kupheh

full Irish breakfast
bricféasta Gaelach iomlán
brickfawsta Gayle-ock umlawn

garlic potatoes
prátaí gairleoige
pratee gar-lyoga

garlic
gairleog
garlyowg

gherkin
gircín
girkeen

goose
gé
gay

130

Menu reader

grapefruit
seadóg
shadowg

green pepper
piobar glas
pibbar glass

grilled meat
feoil ghríostha
fyowl ggreeska

grilled tuna
tuna gríosctha
tuna greeska

haggis
hagaois
hagaysh

hake fillet
colmóir filléid
kulmore fillayje

hake in parsley sauce
colmóir in anraith peirsile
kulmore in onreeh pershila

ice cream
uachtar reoite
ooktar rowcha

. . . in sauce
le anraith
leh onreeh

jam
subh milis
soo milish

lamb chop
gríscín uaineola
greeshkeen oonowla

leeks
cainninne
kaninneh

lemon
liomóid
lyumowje

lettuce
leitís
leteesh

131

Menu reader

lobster
gliomach
glummock

mackerel
ronnach/ muirlis
runnagh/ murlish

mashed potatoes
brúitín
brootcheen

meat stew with vegetables
stobhach feola le glasraí
stowakh fyowla leh glassree

meat
feoil
fyowl

meatballs
feoilmheallta
fyowl-vallta

melon
mealbhacán
mallvakawn

mint
mismín
mishmeen

mixed salad
sailéad measctha
shallayje masska

mushrooms
beacán / beacáin (pl.)
backawn / backawin

mushrooms in sauce
beacáin le hanraith
backawin leh hunraih

mushrooms with garlic
beacáin le gairleog
backawin leh garlowge

mussels
diúilicín / diúilicíní (pl.)
julleekeen / julleekeenee

oil
ola
ola

132

olives
ológa
ologa

onions
oinniún / oinniúin (pl.)
unnyoon / unnyoo-in

oranges
oráistí
orawshtee

oysters
oisrí
oyshree

parsley
peirsil
pershil

parsnip
meacán bán
makan bawn

peach
péitseog
paytshawg

pear
piorra
pirra

peas
pis / piseanna (pl.)
peesh / peeshinna

pheasant
piasún
pee-asoon

pineapple
anann
anann

plums
pluma / plumaí (pl.)
plumma / plummee

pomegranate
pomagrainít
pommagraneet

pork chops
gríscíní muiceola
greeshkeenee mwickowla

Menu reader

pork roast
muiceoil rósta
mwickowl rowsta

pork sausage
ispín muiceola
ispeen mwickowla

potato salad
sailéad prataí / fataí
shallayje prawtee / fottee

potatoes
prátaí
prawtee

pudding
maróg
marowg

raspberries
sú chraobh/súnna chraobh
(pl.)
soo krayve / soonna krayve

red pepper
piobar dearg
pibbar djarrig

rib eye of beef
'rib-eye' mairteola
rib-eye more-chowla

rice pudding
maróg ríse
marowg reesha

roast apple
úll rósta
oo-ill rawsta

roast beef
mairteoil rósta
marchowl rowsta

roast chicken
sicín rósta
shickeen rowsta

roast duck
lachan rósta
lokken rowsta

roast lamb
uaineoil rósta
ooanowle rowsta

roast potatoes
prátaí rósta
prawtee rowsta

salad
sailéad
shallayje

sandwich
ceapaire
kyapairah

sauté potatoes
prátaí friochta
prawtee frikhta

scrambled eggs
uibheacha scrofa
ivaka skruffa

shallots
seallóid / seallóidí (pl.)
Shallowje / shallowjee

shank (of lamb, etc)
lorga
lurga

smoked mackerel
ronnach deataithe
runnagh dyateeha

smoked salmon
bradán deataithe
bradawn d'yataha

soft boiled egg
ubh scothbhruite
uv skuhvroocha

spaghetti
spaigití
shpagettee

spinach
spionáiste
spyunawshta

sponge cake
císte spúinse
keeshta spoonsha

squid
scuid
skwidge

135

Menu reader

stew
stobhach
stowakh

strawberries and cream
súnna talún agus uachtar
soonna taloon oggus ooktar

strawberries
sú talún / súnna talon (pl.)
soo taloon / soonna taloon

stuffed peppers
piobair líonta
pibbar leenta

sweet corn
min bhuí
min wee

tarragon
dragan
draggan

tongue
teanga
changa

tripe
tríopas
treepas

tuna salad
sailéad tuna
shallayje tuna

turkey
turcaí
turkee

turnip
tornapa
turnapa

veal cutlet
gearrthóg laofheola
gyarrhowge layowla

watercress
biolar
billar

Food allergies

I am allergic to — fish
Tá ailléirge orm le — iasc
Taw awlergeh orum leh — eeask

—shellfish
Tá ailléirge orm le — sliogiasc
Taw awlergeh orum leh — shlug-eeask

— nuts
Tá ailléirge orm le — cnónna
Taw awlergeh orum leh — krowana

— milk
Tá ailléirge orm le — bainne
Taw awlergeh orum leh — bonya

— eggs
Tá ailléirge orm le — uibheacha
Taw awlergeh orum leh — ivvaha

— soy
Tá ailléirge orm le — soighe
Taw awlergeh orum leh — soya

— wheat
Tá ailléirge orm le — cruithneacht
Taw awlergeh orum leh — kri-nucht

— gluten
Tá ailléirge orm le — glútan
Taw awlergeh orum leh — gluten

Wine

Ireland's climate means that it does not have a wine industry of its own, but you will find a huge variety of wines in Irish restaurants. Restaurants will have a red and white house wine, which can be bought by the glass, bottle, or carafe.

Types of wine

medium sweet
measartha milis
mas-ar-ha millish

white
geal
gyall

wine cellar (where wine is made, stored or sold)
siléar fíona
shillare fee-ona

dry
neamh-mhilis
ny-ow villish

light red
dearg éadrom
jarrig aydrum

aged in wood
fágtha in adhmad
fwag-ha in eye-med

sweet
milis
millish

estate-bottled
curtha i mbuidéal san eastát
kurha i muhjayle san estawt

sparkling wine
fíon choipeach
fee-on kuphagh

aperitif
greadóg
gradowge

138

Other drinks

young wine
fíon óg
fee-on oge

rose
rósdath
rose-dohh

medium dry
measartha neamh-mhilis
mas-ar-ha ny-ow villish

red
dearg
darrig

grown and bottled by . . .
arna fhás agus curtha i
mbuidéal ag . . .
*arna oss oggus kurha i
muhjayle egg*

**wine made by the
Champagne method**
fíon déanta i modh
seaimpéin
*fee-on djanta i mowe
shampayne*

Other drinks

apple brandy
branda úill
bronda oo-ill

apple juice
sú úll
soo oo-ill

apricot juice
sú aibreog
soo abrowg

beer
beoir / leann
b'yore / ylann

bottled beer
buidéal beorach
bujayle byore-agh

a large beer
beoir mhór
b'yore vore

139

Other drinks

a small glass of draught beer
gloine bheag de bheoir bhairille
glinnya vug de vyore varilla

brandy
branda
bronda

a brandy
branda
bronda

camomile tea
tae fíogadáin
tay feegadawn

canned beer
canna beorach
kanna byore-agh

cappuccino
cappuccino
cappuccino

champagne
seaimpéin
sham-payne

cherry brandy
branda silín
bronda shilleen

cider
fíon úll
fee-on oo-il

coca-cola
coca-cola
coca cola

coffee with a dash of milk
caife le rud beag bainne
kafay leh rud bug bonya

coffee with a dash of brandy
caife le rud beag branda
kafay leh rud bug bronda

coffee with ice cream
caife le huachtar reoite
kafay le h ookhtar rowcha

coffee with whiskey
caife le huisce beatha
kafay le hishka bahha

coffee
caife
kafay

decaffeinated coffee
caife saoi ó chaiféin
kafay decaf

Gaelic coffee (=Irish coffee but with more whiskey)
Caife Gaelach
Kafay ayrinnagh

iced coffee
caife reoite
kafay rowcha

instant coffee
caife ar an toirt
kafay air un turch

Irish coffee
Caife Éireannach
Kafay ayrinnagh

large black coffee
caife dubh mór
kafay doo more

small black coffee
caife dubh beag
kafay duv byug

white coffee
caife le bainne
kafay leh bonya

fruit cup with wine
sailéad torthaí le fíon
sall-yed torhee leh fee-on

a glass of red wine
gloine fíona dheirg
glinna fee-ona yerrig

a glass of white wine
gloine fíona bháin
glinna fee-ona wawn

grape juice
sú fíonchaor
soo feen-heer

lemon tea
tae líomóide
tay l'yeemowdja

Other drinks

lemonade
líomanáid
l'yeemanawdje

liqueur
licéar
likare

mineral water
uisce mianrach
ishka meenra

orange drink
deoch oráiste
jawkh orawshta

orange juice
sú oráistí
soo orawsht-ee

peach juice
sú péitseog
soo paytshowg

soda water
uisce sóide
ishka sowdja

soya milk
bainne soighe
bonya soya

stout
leann dubh
lann duv

tea
tae
tay

tea with milk
tae le bainne
tay leh bonya

tonic water
uisce athbhríoch
ishka ahhvree-ock

OUT AND ABOUT

The weather

Irish weather is notoriously variable, so be prepared for rain, even on a warm and sunny day. Otherwise, the weather is temperate, usually not too hot in summer or overly cold in winter. Bad storms and heavy snow are very rare. High summer temperatures rarely top 28 degrees Celsius, but be prepared for the sun. Cool breezes can be deceptive, especially near the sea, and you can get badly sunburnt before you realise how strong the sun really is.

Is it going to get any warmer?
An éireoidh sé níos teo?
Un neye-row-hee shay neess chaw

Is the weather going to stay like this?
An leanfaidh an aimsir mar seo?
Un lyanhee un amshir mar shuh

Is there going to be a thunderstorm?
An mbeidh spéirling ann?
Un meye spare-lying unn

The weather

Isn't it a lovely day?
Nach bréa an lá é?
Nah braw un law ay

It has stopped snowing
Stop an sneachta
Stup un snyagh-cha

It is a very clear night
Is oíche gheal í
Iss eeha yal ee

It is far too hot
Tá sé i bhfad ró-the
Taw shay i wodd row-heh

It is foggy
Tá ceo ann
Taw kyaw unn

It is raining again
Tá sé ag cur báistí arís
*Taw shay egg kur bawshtee
areesh*

It is very cold
Tá sé an-fhuar
Taw shay un oor

It is very windy
Tá sé an-ghaofar
Taw shay un gweefar

There is a cool breeze
Tá siorradh fuar ann
Taw shirr-oo foor unn

What is the temperature?
Cad é an teocht
Cad-jay un chawght

It is going to be fine
Beidh ségo bréa
Beye shay guh braw

It's going to be windy
Beidh sé gaofar
Beye shay gweefar

It's going to rain
Beidh báisteach ann
Beye bwash-chah unn

It's going to snow
Beidh sneachta ann
Beye shnyagh-ta unn

On the beach

Will it be cold tonight?
An mbéidh sé fuar anocht?
Un meye shay foor anaught

Will the weather improve?
An éireoidh an aimsir níos fearr?
Un nyeye-row-hee un am-shir neess farr

Will the wind die down?
An síothlóidh an gaoth?
Un shee-loe-ee un ghee

On the beach

Can we change here?
An bhféadfaimis athrú anseo?
Un vayd-fameesh ahroo unshoh

Can you recommend a quiet beach?
An dtig leat trá chiúin a mholadh?
Un djig lyat traw hyoon a woll-oo

Is it safe to swim here?
An bhfuil sé sábháilte snámh anseo?
Un will shay sa-wawlt-cha snow unshoh

Is the current strong?
An bhfuil an sruth láidir?
Un will un sruh lawjir

145

On the beach

Is the sea calm?
An bhfuil an fharraige socair?
Un will un arrigga sucker

      Can I rent — a sailing boat?
An bhféadfainn bád — seoil a fháil ar cíos?
Un vayd-finn bawd — showil a ile er keess

      — a rowing boat?
An bhféadfainn bád — iomartha a fháil ar cíos?
Un vayd-finn bawd — umarha a ile er keess

Is it possible to go — sailing?
An bhféadfaí — dul ag seoltóireacht?
Un vayd-fee — dull egg showle-torokt

      — surfing?
An bhféadfaí — dul ag marcaíocht toinne?
Un vayd-fee — dull egg markayokt tinnya

      — water skiing?
An bhféadfaí — sciáil uisce a dhéanamh
Un vayd-fee — shkee-awl ishka a yaynoo

      — wind surfing?
An bhféadfaí — dul ag marcaíocht gaoithe?
Un vayd-fee — dull egg mark-ee-oght gweeha

Is the water warm?
An bhfuil an t-uisce te?
Un will un tishka teh

Sport and recreation

Is there a heated swimming pool?
An bhfuil linn snámha téite ann?
Un will lyinn snawa taycha unn

Is there a lifeguard here?
An bhfuil garda coirp anseo?
Un will gorda kirp unshoh

Is this beach private?
An trá phríobháideach í seo?
Un traw freevawjah ee shuh

When is high tide?
Cathain a bhíonn sé lán?
Kohhen a vee-on shay lawn

When is low tide?
Cathain a bhíonn lag trá ann?
Kohhen a vee-on log traw unn

Sport and recreation

Can I rent the equipment?
An bhféadfainn an trealamh a fháil ar cíos?
Un vayd-hinn un trall-oo a ile er keess

Can we	— go riding?
An bhféadfaimis	— dul ag marcaíocht?
Un vayd-ameesh	*— dull egg markayoght*

147

Entertainment

Can we	**— play tennis?**
An bhféadfaimis	— leadóg a imirt?
Un vayd-ameesh	*— lyadoge a imirch*

	— play golf?
An bhféadfaimis	— galf a imirt?
Un vayd-ameesh	*— galf a imirch*

	— play volleyball?
An bhféadfaimis	— eitpheil a imirt?
Un vayd-ameesh	*— etch-fell a imirch*

Where can we fish?
Cá háit a bhféadfaimis iascaireacht a dhéanamh?
Kaw hawtch a vayd-ameesh eeskaroght a yannoo

Do we need a permit?
An mbeidh ceadúnas uainn?
Un meye k'yadoonass oo-inn

Entertainment

How much is it for a child?
Cad é an táille do pháiste?
Kad jay un tall-ye duh fawshta

How much is it per person?
Cad é an táille do gach duine?
Kad jay an tall-ye duh gah dinnya

Entertainment

How much is it to get in?
Cad é an táille?
Kad jay an tall-ye

  Is there — a disco?
An bhfuil — dioscó ann?
  Un will — jisco unn

      — a good nightclub?
An bhfuil — club oíche maith ann?
  Un will — klub eeha mah unn

      — a theatre?
An bhfuil — amharclann ann?
  Un will — owwerklonn unn

Are there any comedies?
An bhfuil scannán grinn ann?
Un will skanawn grin unn

Two tickets for the late show, please
Dhá thicéad seó mall, le do thoil
Gaw hickayde dun show moll leh duh hull

Two tickets, please
Dhá thicéad, le do thoil
Gaw hickayde leh duh hull

Is there a reduction for children?
An bhfuil lacáiste ann do pháistí?
Un will lock-awsh-ta unn duh fawshtee

149

Sightseeing

Are there any boat trips on the river?
An bhfuil turas báid ar an abhainn?
Un will turras bawje er on owwen

Are there any guided tours of the castle?
An bhfuil turas treoraithe sa chaisleán?
Un will turras chraw-ree-ha sa hashlawn

Are there any guided tours?
An bhfuil turas treoraithe ann?
Un will turras chraw-ree-ha unn

What is there to see here?
Cad é atá le feiceáil anseo?
Kaf jay ataw le feckawl unshoh

What is this building?
Cén foirgneamh é seo?
Kayun furgniv ay shuh

When was it built?
Cathain a tógadh é?
Kohhen a towge-oo ay

150

Sightseeing

Is it open to the public?
An bhfuil sé ar oscailt don phobal?
Un will shay air usk-iltch dun fubbel

What is the admission charge?
Cad é an táille?
Kad jay un tall-ya

Can we go in?
An bhfuil cead isteach againn?
Un will k'yad iss-chah uginn

Can we go up to the top?
An bhféadfaimis dul suas go dtí an barr?
Un vayd-hameesh dull soo-ass guh djee un borr

Can I take photos?
An bhfuil cead agam grianghraif a ghlacadh?
Un will k'yad aggum greengrif a lock-oo

Can I use a flash?
An bhfuil cead agam splanc a úsáid?
Un will k'yad aggum splunk a oosawje

How long does the tour take?
Cá fhad a thógann an turas?
Kaw hodd a howge-ann un turras

Is there a guide book?
An bhfuil eolaí ann?
Un will ole-ee unn

Souvenirs

Is there a tour of the cathedral?
An bhfuil turas na hardeaglaise ann?
Un will turras na hard-uglish-eh unn

Is there an Irish-speaking guide?
An bhfuil treoraí Gaeilge ann?
Un will chroaree Gaylick unn

Is this the best view?
An é seo an radharc is fearr?
Un ay shoh un reye-arc iss farr

What time does the gallery open?
Cathain a osclaíonn an dánlann?
Kohhen a usklee-on un dawnlonn

When is the bus tour?
Cathain atá an turas bus?
Kohhen ataw un turras bus

Souvenirs

Have you got an English guidebook?
An bhfuil eolaí Béarla agaibh?
Un will oal-ee bair-la agiv

Have you got any colour slides?
An bhfuil sleamhnáin dhaite agaibh?
Un will shlowe-noyne gotcha agiv

Going to church

Where can I buy postcards?
Cá háit is féidir cártaí poist a cheannach?
Kaw hawtch is faydge-urr kortee pwisht a khyanna

Where can we buy souvenirs?
Cá háit a bhféadfaimis cuimhneacháin a cheannach?
Kaw hawtch a vayd-hameesh wivnehoyne a khyanna

Going to church

The most common religion in Ireland is Catholicism, but most towns will also have a Church of Ireland and Presbyterian church. Most churches will be open throughout the day so you may visit the church by yourself or enquire about the times of church services. There are also several mosques and synagogues in Ireland, most of which are in Dublin. 'Séipéal' usually refers to a Catholic church whereas 'eaglais' and 'teampall' are more often used for Protestant churches.

Where is the — Catholic church?
Cá bhfuil an — séipéal Caitliceach?
Kaw will on — shaypayle catch-lick-ah

— Baptist church?
Cá bhfuil an — eaglais Bhaisteach?
Kaw will on — uglish wash-chah

Going to church

Where is the — mosque?
Cá bhfuil an — mosc?
Kaw will on — mosk

— Protestant church?
Cá bhfuil an — eaglais Phrotastúnach
Kaw will on — uglish frotastoonah

— synagogue?
Cá bhfuil an — tsionagóg?
Kaw will on — chunna-gowge

What time is mass?
Cathain a bhíonn aifreann ann?
Kohhen a vee-on afrin unn

I would like to see a priest
Ba mhaith liom sagart a fheieáil
Buh wah lyum sogart a eckawl

I would like to see a minister
Ba mhaith liom ministir a fheiceáil
Buh wah lyum minish-chur a eckawl

I would like to see a rabbi
Ba mhaith liom raibí a fheiceáil
Buh wah lyum rabbee a eckawl

SHOPPING

The main cities in Ireland can contain treasure troves of bargains for the avid shopper with independent retailers particular to the area, as well as the major high street chains you'd also find in Britain. Many small towns will have local clothing or craft shops which can contain both bargains and unique items for sale. Shops in cities and towns will open from 9am to 6pm and will often open until 9pm on Thursdays. Some newsagents and convenience stores in towns and cities may stay open past midnight. Christmas time and the winter sales see the shops often open longer. Summer sales take place in June and July and are an oasis for bargain hunters.

Many towns have a market one day per week with a wide range of goods on sale, including fruit, fish, clothes and cheap electrical goods. It is worthwhile asking locally when the markets are on when one reaches a town. Nowadays petrol stations have taken over the role of local shops and they pride themselves on their wide range of goods on sale. Almost every small town will have a chemist ('poitigéir'/ 'cógaslann'), corner shop ('siopa') where groceries and newspapers are available and sometimes a bakery, 'bacús'. Alcohol and cigarettes are generally available in larger shops as well as specialist off-licenses 'eascheadúnas'. Plastic bags are taxed to encourage shoppers to re-use old ones.

General phrases and requests

How much does that cost?
Cá mhéad atá air sin?
Kaw vayd ataw er shin

How much is it — per kilo?
Cá mhéad atá ar — chileagram?
Kaw vayd ataw air — hilagram

— per metre?
Cá mhéad atá ar — mhéadar?
Kaw vayd ataw air — vaydar

How much is this?
Cá mhéad atá air seo?
Kaw vayd ataw air shuh

Have you got anything cheaper?
An bhfuil rud níos saoire agat?
Un will rud neess seera ugut

Can I see that umbrella?
An bhféadfainn an scáth fearthainne sin a fheiceáil
Un vayd-hing un skoh farhannya shin ah eckawl

No, the other one
Ní an ceann sin. An ceann eile
Nee un kyunn shuin. un kyunne ella

General phrases and requests

Can you deliver to my hotel?
An bhféadfá é a chur chuig m'óstán?
Un vayd-haw ay a hur higg muh owstawn

I do not like it
Ní maith liom é
Nee mah lyum ay

I like this one
Is maith liom an ceann seo
Iss mah lyum un kyunn shuh

I will take — this one
Tógfaidh mé — an ceann seo
Towg-ay may— un kyunn shuh

— that one
Tógfaidh mé — an ceann sin
Towg-ay may — un kyunn shin

— the other one
Tógfaidh mé — an ceann eile
Towg-ay may — un kyunn ella

— that one over there
Tógfaidh mé — an ceann thall ansin
Towg-hee may— on kyunn holl unshin

Where can I buy some clothes?
Cá háit a bhféadfainn éadaí a cheannach
Kaw hawch a vayd-hinn aydee ah khyannah

General phrases and requests

Where can I buy tapes for my camcorder?
Cá háit a bhféadfainn téipeanna do m'fhíscheamara a fháil
Kaw hawch vayd-hinn chaypanna duh meeshkhyamara ah ile

Where can I get my camcorder repaired?
Cá háit a bhféadfainn m'fhíscheamara a fháil deisithe
Kaw hawch a vayd-hing meesh-khyamara a ile yesh-eeha

Where is — the children's department?
Cá bhfuil — roinn na bpáistí?
Kaw will — rinn na bawsh-chee

— the food department?
Cá bhfuil — an roinn bia?
Kaw will — un rinn bee

I am looking for a souvenir
Tá mé ag lorg cuimhneacháin
Taw may egg lurg kivnya-hoyne

Do you sell sunglasses?
An ndíolann sibh spléaclaí gréine?
Un nyeelann shiv spayklee greynyeh

Can I have a carrier bag?
An dtig liom mála a fháil
Un jig lyum mawla a ile

Can I have a receipt?
An bhféadfainn admháil a fháil?
Un vayd-hinn adwawl a ile

158

General phrases and requests

Can I have an itemised bill?
An bhféadfainn bille leis na sonraí a fháil
Un vayd-hinn bill-ya lyesh na sunree a ile

Can I pay for air insurance?
An bhféadfainn íoc as árachas aeir?
Un vayd-hinn eek os arahas air

What is the total?
Cad é an t-iomlán?
Cad jay an chumlunn

Do you accept traveller's cheques?
An nglacann sibh le seiceanna taistil?
Un n-lakann shiv le sheckinna tash-chill

I do not have enough euros
Níl go leor euro agam
Nyeel guh lyore euro ugum

I do not have enough money
Níl go leor airgid agam
Nyeel guh lyore arrigidge ugum

I would like to pay with my credit card
Ba mhaith liom íoc as le mo chárta creidmheasa
Buh wah lyum eek oss leh muh khorta kredvassa

Please forward a receipt to this address
Seol admháil chuig an seoladh seo, le do thoil
Showle adwawl hig un showla shoh, leh duh hull

Buying groceries

Please wrap it up for me
Burláil e dom, le do thoil
Burlawl ay doo, leh duh hull

There is no need to wrap it
Níl ort é a bhurláil
Nyeel urt ay a wurlawl

Please pack this for shipment
Pacáil é seo le haghaigh seoladh
Pakawl ay shaw le hihe showla

Will you send it by air freight?
An seolfaidh tú é trí aerphost?
Un showlhee too ay tchree airfust

Buying groceries

Groceries can of course be bought from supermarkets but, for the best quality, and for a bit of local flavour why not try independent traders. Try farmer's markets and local butchers, bakers and greengrocers to get a taste of locally sourced produce and also support the local economy. For more specialised food items, there are also a few gourmet food markets and ethnic food shops.

We need to buy some food
Tá orainn bia a cheannach
Taw ureenn bee-ah a khyannah

Buying groceries

I would like — a kilo of potatoes
Ba mhaith liom — cileagram prátaí
Buh wah lyum — kilagram prawtee

— a bar of chocolate
Ba mhaith liom — barra seacláide
Buh wah lyum — barra shoklodja

— 100 g of coffee
Ba mhaith liom — céad gram caife
Buh wah lyum — kayd gram kafay

— two steaks
Ba mhaith liom — dhá stéig
Buh wah lyum — gaw shtayg

— five slices of ham
Ba mhaith liom — cúig shlisín liamháis
Buh wah lyum — koo-ig h-lisheen lyeewawsh

— half a dozen eggs
Ba mhaith liom — leathdhosaen uibh
Buh wah lyum — ly-ah-ghusane ivv

— half a kilo of butter
Ba mhaith liom — leathchileagram ime
Buh wah lyum — ly-ah-khilagram immeh

Can I have — some sugar, please?
An bhféadfainn — siúcra a fháil, le do thoil?
Un vayd-hinn — shookra a ile, leh duh hull

Groceries

Can I have — a bottle of wine, please?
An bhféadfainn — buidéal fíona a fháil, le do thoil?
Un vayd-hinn — bujayle fee-ona a ile, leh duh hull

— a kilo of sausages, please?
An bhféadfainn — cileagram ispíní a fháil, le do thoil?
Un vayd-hinn — kilagram ishpeenee a ile, leh duh hull

— a leg of lamb, please?
An bhféadfainn — ceathrú uaineola a fháil le do thoil?
Un vayd-hinn — kyahhroo oonowla a ile, leh duh hull

— a litre of milk, please?
An bhféadfainn — líotar bainne a fháil, le do thoil?
Un vayd-hinn — lyeetar bonya a ile, leh duh hull

Groceries

baby food
bia linbh
bee-ah lyinn-yiv

butter
im
im

biscuits
brioscaí
briskee

cheese
cáis
kawsh

bread
arán
arawn

coffee
caife
kafay

162

cream
uachtar
ooghtar

eggs
uibheacha
ivvaha

flour
plúr
ploor

jam
subh
soo

margarine
buíoc
bwee-ok

milk
bainne
bonya

mustard
mustard
mustard

oil
ola
ulla

pepper
piobar
pibbar

rice
rís
reesh

salt
salann
solann

soup
anraith
onreeh

sugar
siúcra
shookra

tea
tae
tay

vinegar
fínéagar
feenaygar

yoghurt
iógart
yoghurt

Meat and fish

beef
mairteoil
mar-chowle

chicken
sicín
shikeen

cod
trosc
trusk

fish
iasc
eesk

ham
liamhás
ly-eewaws

herring
scadán
skodawn

kidneys
duáin
doo-oyne

lamb
uaineoil
oon-yowle

liver
ae
ay

meat
feoil
f'yowle

mussels
diúilicíní
jullekeenee

pork
muiceoil
muk-yowle

sole
sól
sole

veal
laofheoil
layowl

164

At the newsagent's

Do you sell — paperbacks?
An ndíolann sibh — leabhair faoi chlúdach bog?
Un nyeelann shiv — lyower fwee h-loo-dah bug

— postcards?
An ndíolann sibh — cártaí poist?
Un nyeelann shiv — kortee pwisht

— a local map?
An ndíolann sibh — léarscáil áitiúil
Un nyeelann shiv — lyare-skawl awtchool

— a road map?
An díolann sibh — léarscáil bhóithre
Un nyeelann shiv — lyare-skawl woyhra

— coloured pencils?
An ndíolann sibh — pinn luaidhe dhaite
Un nyeelann shiv — pin loo-wee gotcha

— drawing paper?
An ndíolann sibh — páipéar ealaíne
Un nyeelann shiv — pawpayre aleena

— markers?
An díolann sibh — pinn dhaite
Un nyeelann shiv — pin gotcha

165

At the newsagent's

Do you sell — street maps?
An ndíolann sibh — léarscáileanna sráide
Un nyeelann shiv — lare-skawlanna srodya

I would like some postage stamps
Ba mhaith liom roinnt stampaí poist
Buh wah lyum rintch stompee pwisht

Do you have any books in Irish?
An bhfuil leabhar ar bith i nGaeilge agaibh
Un will lyower air bee ing-ay-lig agiv

Do you have English newspapers?
An bhfuil nuachtáin Shasanacha agaibh
Un will noo-toyne hasanaha agiv

I need some writing paper
Tá páipéar litreach uaim
Taw pawpayre litch-rah woom

I need a bottle of ink
Tá buidéal dúigh uaim
Taw budjayle dooee woom

I need a pen
Tá peann uaim
Taw pan woom

I need a pencil
Tá peann luaidhe uaim
Taw pan loo-ee woom

I need some adhesive tape
Tá gléthéip uaim
Taw glyay-hape woom

I need some envelopes
Tá clúdaigh uaim
Taw kloodee woom

At the tobacconist's

Do you have — cigarette papers?
An bhfuil — páipéar toitíní agat
Un will — pawpayre titcheenee ugut

— a box of matches
An bhfuil — bosca cipíní agat
Un will — buksa kipeenee ugut

— a cigar
An bhfuil — todóg agat
Un will — todowg ugut

— a cigarette lighter
An bhfuil — lastóir toitíní agat
Un will — lastore titcheenee ugut

— a gas (butane) refill
An bhfuil — athlíonadh gáis agat
Un will — ohhlyeenoo gowsh ugut

167

At the tobacconist's

Do you have — a pipe
An bhfuil — píopa agat
Un will — peepa ugut

— a pouch of pipe tobacco
An bhfuil — mealbhóg tobac píopa agat
Un will — mall-woge tubak peepa ugut

— some pipe cleaners
An bhfuil — réiteoirí píopa agat
Un will — raychoree peepa ugut

Have you got — any American brands?
An bhfuil — brandaí Meiriceánach agat
Un will — brondee Merakawnaha ugut

— any English brands?
An bhfuil — brandaí Sasanacha agat
Un will — brondee sasanaha ugut

— rolling tobacco?
— tobac scaoilte
— tubak skeeltcha

A packet of . . . — please
Paicéad . . . — le do thoil
Pakayde . . . — leh duh hull

— with filter tips
— le scagairí
— le scagaree

At the chemist's

A packet of . . . — without filters
  Paicéad . . . — gan scagairí
  Pakayde . . . — gon scagaree

At the chemist's

Chemist's and pharmacies usually have the same opening hours as most shops, but you will find some late night chemist's in cities and large towns. They will sell anything from cough medicine to bandages, but like British pharmacies, some drugs may only be bought with a prescription from a doctor.

Do you have toothpaste?
An bhfuil taos fiacla agat
Un will tayss feekla agut

I need some high-protection suntan cream
Tá lois griandaite láidir uaim
Taw lish greendotcha loyjir oom

Can you give me something for — a headache?
An bhféadfá rud éigin a thabhairt dom i gcóir — tinneas cinn
Un vayd-faw rud aygin a hoo-ert dum ee gore — tinnass keen

— insect bites?
An bhféadfá rud éigin a thabhairt dom i gcóir — plaiceanna
                                                feithidí
*Un vayd-faw rud aygin a hoo-ert dum ee gore — plakinna
                                                fehiddee*

169

At the chemist's

Can you give me something for — a cold?
An bhféadfá rud éigin a thabhairt dom i gcóir — slaghdán
Un vayd-faw rud aygin a hoo-ert dum ee gore — sly-dawn

— a cough
An bhféadfá rud éigin a thabhairt dom i gcóir — casacht
Un vayd-faw rud aygin a hoo-ert dum ee gore — kosokt

— a sore throat
An bhféadfá rud éigin a thabhairt dom i gcóir — scornach
tinn
*Un vayd-faw rud aygin a hoo-ert dum ee gore — skornok
teen*

— an upset stomach
An bhféadfá rud éigin a thabhairt dom i gcóir — bolg tinn
Un vayd-faw rud aygin a hoo-ert dum ee gore — bulg teen

— toothache
An bhféadfá rud éigin a thabhairt dom i gcóir — tinneas
fiacla
*Un vayd-faw rud aygin a hoo-ert dum ee gore — tinnass
feekla*

— hay fever
An bhféadfá rud éigin a thabhairt dom i gcóir — fiabhras
léana
*Un vayd-faw rud aygin a hoo-ert dum ee gore — feevras
layanna*

Medicines and toiletries

Can you give me something for — sunburn
An bhféadfá rud éigin a thabhairt dom i gcóir — craiceann
griandóite
*Un vayd-faw rud aygin a hoo-ert dum ee gore — krakinn
greendowtcha*

Do I need a prescription?
An bhfuil oideas dochtúra uaim
Un will ijass duktoora oom

How many do I take?
Cé mhéad gur ceart dom a thógáil?
Kay vayd gur k'yart dum a howgawle

How often do I take them?
Cé chomh minic is ceart dom iad a thógáil
Kay kow minik is k'yart dum eed a howgawle

Are they safe for children to take?
An bhfuil siad sábhálta do pháistí?
Un will sheed saw-walcha duh fawshtee

Medicines and toiletries

antiseptic
frithsheipteach
frihhsheptok

aspirin
aspairín
aspareen

171

Medicines and toiletries

bandage
bindealán
bindalawn

cleansing milk
lois ghlantach
lish glontok

conditioner
feabhsóir gruaige
f'yowsore groo-igeh

condom
coiscín
kishkeen

contraceptive
frithghiniúnach
frihhginoonok

cotton wool
olann chadáis
ulann khodawsh

deodorant
díbholaíoch
deevullee-cok

disinfectant
díghalrán
deegolrawn

eye shadow
smideadh súile
smijjeh sooleh

face powder
púdar aghaidhe
poodore eye-geh

hair spray
sprae gruaige
spray groo-igeh

hand cream
lois láimhe
lish loyva

laxative
purgóid
purgoje

lipstick
béaldath
bayle-dohh

mascara
mascára
maskora

moisturiser
taisritheoir
tashrihore

172

Medicines and toiletries

mouthwash
folcadh béil
fulk-ha bayle

nail file
líomhán iongan
leevawn ungan

nail varnish
vearnais iongan
varnish ungan

nail varnish remover
díothóir vearnais iongan
dee-ohore varnish ungan

perfume
cumhrán
koove-rawn

plasters
greimlíní
grime-leenee

razor blades
colganna rásúir
kulganna rawsoor

sanitary towels
tuaillí slaintíochta
too-awlyee slawntee-ockta

shampoo
foltfholcadh
fultfulk-ha

shaving cream
gallúnach bhearrtha
galloonock varrha

soap
gallúnach
galloonock

suntan lotion
lois griandaite
lish greendotcha

talc
talcam
talkam

tampons
súitíní
soocheenee

tissues
ciarsúir páipéir
keersoor pawpayre

toothpaste
taos fiacla
tayss feekla

Shopping for clothes

I am just looking, thank you
Nílim ach ag féachaint orthu, go raibh maith agat
Nyeelim ok egg faykant urhoo, guh row mah agut

I do not like it
Ní maith liom é
Nee mah lyum ay

I like it
Is maith liom é
Iss mah lyum ay

I will take it
Tógfaidh mé é
Towghee may ay

	I like — this one
Is maith liom	— an ceann seo
Is mah lyum	— *un k'yowne shoh*

	— that one there
Is maith liom	— an ceann thall ansin
Iss mah lyum	— *un k'yowne holl unshin*

	— the one in the window
Is maith liom	— an ceann san fhuinneog
Iss mah lyum	— *un k'yowne san innyowg*

174

Shopping for clothes

I would like — this suit
Ba mhaith liom — an culaith seo
Buh wah lyum — un kullee shih

— this hat
Ba mhaith liom — an hata seo
Buh wah lyum — un hotta shoh

I would like one — with a zip
Ba mhaith liom ceann — le sip
Buh wah lyum k'yowne — leh sip

— without a belt
Ba mhaith liom ceann — gan chrios
Buh wah lyum k'yowne — gon khrish

Can you please measure me?
An bhféadfá mo thomhas a thógáil?
Un vayd-faw muh howish a howgawle

Can I change it if it does not fit?
An bhféadfaidh mé é a athrú muna bhfuil mo thomhas
ceart ann
*Un vayd-hee may ay a ahroo munna will muh howish
k'yart unn*

Have you got this in other colours?
An bhfuil an ceann seo agat i ndathanna eile
Un will un k'yowne shoh agut ih nahanna ella

Shopping for clothes

I take a large shoe size
Tá tomhas bróige móire agam
Taw towish browgeh moora agum

Is it too long?
An bhfuil sé rófhada?
Un will shay row-odda

Is it too short?
An bhfuil sé róghearr?
Un will shay row-g'yarr

Is there a full-length mirror?
An bhfuil scathán ard anseo
Un will skoh-hawn ord unshoh

Is this all you have?
An é sin an méid atá agat?
Un ay shin un mayd ataw agut

It does not fit
Níl mo thomhas ceart ann
Nyeel muh how-ass k'yart unn

It does not suit me
Ní oireann sé dom
Nee irrin shay dum

May I see it in daylight?
An bhféadfainn é a fheicéail le solas na gréine?
Un vayd-hinn ay shin ah eckawl leh sullas na graynyeh

Shopping for clothes

Where are the changing (dressing) rooms?
Cá bhfuil na seomraí gléasta?
Kaw will na showmree glaysta

Where can I try it on?
Cá háit go bhféadfainn é a chur orm?
Kaw hawtch guh vayd-hinn ay ah khur urm

Have you got — a large size?
 An bhfuil — tomhas mór agat?
  Un will — tow-ass moor agut

    — a small size?
 An bhfuil — tomhas beag agat?
  Un will — tow-ass b'yug agut

What is it made of?
Cad é ábhar an rud seo?
Kad ay aw-ver un rud shoh

Is it guaranteed?
An bhfuil bannaí leis?
Un will bannee lesh

Will it shrink?
An giortóidh sé?
Un g'yirtowee shay

Is it drip-dry?
An bhfuil sé 'drip-dry'
Un will shay 'drip dry'

177

Clothes and accessories

Is it dry-clean only?
An mbeidh orm é a thirimghlanadh?
Un meye urm ay ah hirringhlonna

Is it machine washable?
An mbeidh mé in ann é a ní sa mheaisín níocháin
Un meye may in unn ay ah nee sa vasheen nee-ukawn

Clothes and accessories

belt
crios
krish

blouse
blús
blooss

bra
cíochbheart
kee-okvart

bracelet
braisléad
brashlayde

brooch
dealgan
jalgawn

button
cnapa
k'napa

cardigan
cairdeagan
cardigan

coat
cóta
kowta

178

Clothes and accessories

corduroy
corda an rí
korda un ree

cotton
cadás
kodaws

denim
deinim
jenim

dress
gúna
goona

dungarees
bríste dungaraí
breeshteh dungaree

earrings
fáinní cluaise
fawnee cloosheh

fur
fionnadh / clúmh
f'yunna / kloov

gloves
láimhíní
lawveenee

handbag
mála láimhe
mawla loyveh

handkerchief
ciarsúr
keersoor

hat
hata
hotta

jacket
seacáid
shackayde

jeans
bríste deinime
breeshteh jenimeh

jersey
geansaí
ganzee

lace
lása
lawsa

leather
leathair
lahher

179

Clothes and accessories

linen
línéadach
leenayjock

necklace
muince
m'winkeh

nightdress
léine oíche
layneh eeha

nylon
níolón
nee-olowne

pants (women's)
brístíní
breeshteenee

petticoat
peireacót
perrakote

pullover
geansaí
ganzee

purse
sparán
sparawn

pyjamas
pitseámaí
pitshaymee

raincoat
cóta fearthainne
kowta farhenneh

ring
fáinne
fawnyeh

sandals
cuaráin
kooroyne

scarf
scairf
skarf

shirt
léine
layneh

shoes
bróga
browga

shorts
bríste gearrtha
breeshteh g'yarrha

Clothes and accessories

silk
síoda
shee-oda

skirt
sciorta
sk'yurta

slip
foghúna
fowghoona

socks
stocaí
stukkee

stockings
stocaí
stukkee

suede
svaeid
svayd

suit (men's)
culaith
kullee

suit (women's)
culaith
kullee

sweater
geansaí
ganzee

swimming trunks
brístí snámha
breeshtee snawva

swimsuit
culaith snámha
kullee snawva

T-shirt
T-léine
Tee layneh

terylene
teirilín
Cherileen

tie
carbhat
karawot

tights
riteoga
ritchowga

towel
tuáille
too-awlya

Photography

trousers
brístí
breeshtee

umbrella
scath fearthainne
skoh farhenneh

underpants (men's)
fobhrístí
fowvreeshtee

velvet
veilbhit
velvit

vest
veist
vesht

wallet
sparán
sparawn

watch
uaireadóir
ooradore

wool
olann
ulann

zip
sip
sip

Photography

I need a memory card for my digital camera.
Tá cárta cuimhne do mo cheamara digiteach uaim.
Taw kort-ah kiv-neh duh muh chamera dig-it-uch oom

I need a battery for my digital camera.
Tá bataire do mo cheamara digiteach uaim.
Taw batara duh muh chamera dig-it-uch oom

Photography

Where can I print pictures from my digital camera?
Cá háit ar féidir liom grianghraif ó mo cheamara digiteach
a phriontáil?
*Kaw hawch er fayd-jir lyum greengraf oh muh chamera
dig-it-uch ah frint-awl*

I need a film — for this camera
Tá scannán uaim — don cheamara seo
Taw skonnawn oom — dun kh'yamara shoh

— for this camcorder
Tá scannán uaim — don fhíscheamara láimhe seo
Taw skonnawn oom — dun feeshkh'yamara loyveh shoh

Can you develop this film, please?
An bhféadfá an scannán seo a réaladh le do thoil
Un vayd-faw un skonnawn shoh ah rayla le duh hull

I would like this photo enlarged
Tá mé ag iarraidh go mbeidh an grianghraif seo méadaithe
Taw may egg eeree guh meye un greengraf shoh mayde-ihha

I would like two prints of this one
Tá dhá phrionta den cheann seo uaim
Taw gaw frunta dun k'yowne shoh oom

When will the photos be ready?
Cathain a bheidh na grianghraifeanna réidh?
Kohhen ah veye nah green grafinna ray

183

Camera repairs

I want a black and white film
Tá scannán dubh agus bán uaim
Taw skonnawn duv oggus bawn oom

I want batteries for the flash
Tá batairí uaim don splanc
Taw bataree oom dun splank

Camera repairs

I am having trouble with my camera
Tá fadhb agam le mo cheamara
Taw fibe agum leh muh kh'yamara

The film is jammed
Chuaigh an scannán i bhfostú
Koo-ee un skonnawn ih vustu

There is something wrong with my camera
Tá rud éigin mícheart le mo cheamara
Taw rud aygin meek'yart leh muh kh'yamara

Where can I get my camera repaired?
Cá háit go bhféadfaí mo cheamara a dheisiú
Kawtch guh vayd-fee muh kh'yamara a yeshoo

184

Camera parts

accessory
oiriúint
irroonch

blue filter
scagaire gorm
skoggara gurm

camcorder
físcheamara láimhe
feeshkh'yamara loyveh

cartridge
cartús
kortooss

cassette
caiséad
Kashayd

cine-camera
ceamara scannán
k'yamara skonnawn

distance
achar
okker

enlargement
méadú
maydoo

exposure
nochtadh
nukta

exposure meter
méadar nochta
maydar nukta

flash
splanc
splank

focal distance
achar fócásach
okker fowkawsock

focus
fócás
fowkaws

image
iomhá
ee-uvaw

185

Camera parts

in focus
i bhfócás
ih vowkaws

lens cover
clúdach lionsa
kloodock l'yunsa

lens
lionsa
l'yunsa

memory card
cárta cuimhne
kort-ah kiv-neh

negative
claonchló
klayne-khlow

out of focus
as fócas
oss fowkaws

over-exposed
rónochtaithe
rownuktahha

picture
pictiúr
pikchoor

print
prionta
pr'yunta

projector
teilgeoir
chelgore

red filter
scagaire dearg
skoggara darrig

reel
ríl
reel

shade
scáth
skoh

shutter
comhla
kowla

shutter speed
luas comhla
loo-ass kowla

slide
sleamhnán
shl'yownawn

At the hairdresser's

transparency
tréshoilséan
trayhillshawn

tripod
tríchosach
trykussock

viewfinder
lorgán radhairc
lurgawn reye-irk

wide-angle lens
lionsa maoluillinne
l'yunsa m'wale-illinna

yellow filter
scagaire buí
skoggara b'wee

At the hairdresser's

I would like to make an appointment
Ba mhaith liom coinne a shocrú
Buh wah lyum k'winneh a hukroo

I want — a haircut
   Tá — bearradh gruaige uaim
   Taw — barra groo-igeh oom

   — a trim
   Tá — cóiriú gruaige uaim
   Taw — coe-roo groo-igeh woo-im

At the hairdresser's

Not too much off
Ná bain barraíocht
Naw bwin barr-ee-akht

Take a little more off the back
Bain níos mó un gcúl
Bain neess mow own gool

Please cut my hair — short
Bearr mo chuid gruaige — go gairid le do thoil
Barr muh khwidge groo-igeh — guh garidge leh duh hull

— fairly short
Bearr mo chuid gruaige — go measartha gairid le do thoil
Barr muh khwidge groo-igeh — guh massar-hah garidge lehn duh hull

— in a fringe
Bearr mo chuid gruaige — le frainse le do thoil
Barr muh kwidge groo-igeh — leh fransha leh duh hull

That is fine, thank you
Tá sin go breá, go raibh maith agat
Taw shin guh braw guh row mah agut

I would like a perm
An gcuirfeá buantonn i mo chuid gruaige le do thoil?
Un g'wirfaw boo-an-ton ih muh khwidge groo-igeh leh duh hull

188

At the hairdresser's

I would like a blow-dry
Triomaigh mo chuid gruaige le do thoil
Trummee muh khwidge groo-igeh leh duh hull

I would like my hair dyed
An gcuirfeá dath i mo chuid gruaige le do thoil?
Un g'wirfaw dahh ih muh khwidge groo-igeh leh duh hull

I would like my hair streaked
An gcuirfeá stríoca i mo chuid gruaige le do thoil?
Un g'wirfaw stree-ukka ih muh khwidge groo-igeh leh duh hull

I would like a shampoo and cut
An bhféadfá mo chuid gruaige a ní agus a bhearradh le do thoil?
Un vayd-faw muh kwidge groo-igeh ah nee oggus uh varra leh duh hull

I would like a shampoo and set
An bhféadfá mo chuid gruaige a ní agus coirnín a chur ann?
Un vayd-faw muh khwidge groo-igeh a nee oggus korneen a khur unn

I would like a conditioner
Tá feabhsaitheoir gruaige uaim
Taw f'yowsee-hore groo-igeh woo-im

189

Laundry

I would like hairspray
Tá sprae gruaige uaim
Taw spray groo-igeh woo-im

The dryer is too hot
Tá an triomadóir róthe
Taw un trumadore rowheh

The water is too hot
Tá an t-uisce róthe
Taw un tishka rowheh

Laundry

Is there a launderette nearby?
An bhfuil ionad nite éadaí cóngarach don áit seo
Un will unnad nitch-eh aydee kowne-garrakh dun awtch shoh

How does the washing machine work?
Conas a oibríonn an inneall níocháin
Kunass ah ibree-onn un inyall nee-ukhoyne

How long will it take?
Cá fhad a thógfaidh sé?
Kaw odd ah hogey shay

Can you — clean this skirt?
An bhféadfá — an sciorta seo a ní?
Un vayd-faw — un sk'yurta shoh ah nee

Laundry

Can you — clean and press these shirts?
An bhféadfá — na léinte seo a ní agus a phreasáil?
An bhféadfá — nah layncheh shoh ah nee oggus a fressawl

— wash these clothes?
An bhféadfá — na héadaí seo a ní?
An bhféadfá — na haydee shoh ah nee

This stain is oil
Is é ola an cúis an smáil seo
Ishay ulla koosh un smawl shoh

This stain is blood
Is í fuil cúis an smáil seo
Ishee f'will koosh un smawl shoh

This stain is coffee
Is é caife cúis an smáil sco
Ishay kafay koosh un smawl shoh

This stain is ink
Is é dúch cúis an smáil seo
Ishay dookh koosh un smawl shoh

This fabric is delicate
Tá an t-éadach seo fíneálta
Taw un taydakh shoh feenalta

I have lost my dry cleaning ticket
Chaill mé mo thicéad tirimghlanta
Khyle may muh hickayd tirrimghlonta

191

General repairs

Please send it to this address
Cuir chuig an seoladh seo é le do thoil
Kur higg un showla shoh ay leh duh hull

When will I come back?
Cathain ar cheart dom filleadh ar ais?
Kohhen er kh'yart dum filla er ash

When will my clothes be ready?
Cathain a bheidh mo chuid éadaí réidh?
Kohhen ah veye muh khwidge aydee ray

I will come back — later
Tiocfaidh mé ar ais — níos déanaí
Chukkee may er ash — neess djaynee

— in an hour
Tiocfaidh mé ar ais — i gceann uaire
Chukkee may er ash — ih g'yowne oora

General repairs

This is broken
Tá sé seo briste
Taw shay shoh brishta

This is damaged
Tá damáiste déanta don rud seo
Taw damawshteh djanta dun rud shoh

192

This is torn
Tá sé seo stróicthe
Taw shay shoh stroke-ha

Can you repair it?
An bhféadfá é a dheisiú?
Un vayd-faw ay ah yeshoo

Can you do it quickly?
An bhféadfá é a dhéanamh go gasta?
Un vayd-faw ay ah yannoo guh gasta

Have you got a spare part for this?
An bhfuil ball spártha agat do seo?
Un will boll sporha agut duh shoh

Would you have a look at this please?
An bhféachfaidh tú air seo le do thoil?
Un vaykhee too air shoh leh duh hull

Here is the guarantee
Seo é an urrús
Shoh ay un urroos

At the post office

Post offices and postboxes in Ireland will be green and marked An Post or Post Office. Most places, even small

At the post office

villages, will have a post office. Post offices in Ireland offer
a range of services, including banking, as well as the usual
postal services. Postage stamps can sometimes also be
bought in shops or from green vending machines.

12 stamps please
Dhá stampa déag le do thoil
Ghaw stampa djayg leh duh hull

I need to send this by courier
Tá mé ag iarraidh seo a chur le teachtaire
Taw may egg eerree shoh a khur leh tchakhtar-eh

I want to send a telegram
Tá mé ag iarraidh teileagram a sheoladh
Taw may egg eerree tellagram ah h'yowla

I want to send this by registered mail
Ba mhaith liom an rud seo a sheoladh ar phost cláraithe
Buh wah lyum un rud shoh ah h'yowla er fust klore-ihha

I want to send this parcel
Ba mhaith liom an beart seo a sheoladh
Buh wah lyum un bart shoh ah h'yowla

When will it arrive?
Cathain a shroichfidh sé an áit
Kohhen ah hri-hee shay un awtch

194

Using the telephone

How much is a letter — to Europe?
Cá mhéad le litir a chur chun — na hEorpa
Ka vayd leh litchir ah khur hun — *na hawrpa*

— to the United States?
Cá mhéad le litir a chur chun — na Stát Aontaithe
Ka vayd leh litchir ah khur hun — *na stat ayne-teeha*

Six postcard stamps for Europe please
Sé stampa cárta poist don Eoraip le do thoil
Shay stampa karta posht don awrap leh duh hull

Can I have a telegram form, please?
An bhféadfainn foirm teileagraim a fháil le do thoil?
Un vayd-finn fwirrim tellagram ah awl leh duh hull

Using the telephone

Ireland's international dialling code is (353). To ring Ireland, dial 00, then 353, then the area code or mobile phone prefix minus the zero and then the number itself. Similarly, if you are dialling Great Britain, first dial 00 and then 44. Payphones in Ireland may be coin or card operated, and some will accept both. Phonecards can be bought in most newsagents. Directory enquiries in Ireland can be reached at 11850 and 11890.

Using the telephone

Can I use the telephone, please?
An bhféadfainn an teileafón a úsáid le do thoil
Un vayd-finn un tellafone ah oosawje leh duh hull

Can I dial direct?
An féidir glaoch díreach a chur?
Un fay-djir glayokh djeerrakh ah khur

Can you connect me with the international operator?
An bhféadfá mé a chur tríd chiug an oibreoir idirnáisiúnta
*Un vayd-faw may a khur treedj higg un ibrore
iddirnawshoonta*

Have you got any change?
An bhfuil briseadh ar bith agat?
Un will brisha air beeh agut

How do I use the telephone?
Conas a úsáidtear an teileafón?
Kunas ah oosadj-ter an tellafone

How much is it to phone to London?
Cá mhéad atá ar ghlaoch teileafóin go Londain?
Ka vayd ataw air ghlay-okh tellafone guh londan

I must make a phone call to Spain
Tá orm glaoch teileafóin a chur ar an Spáinn
Taw urm glayokh tellafone ah khur er un Spawn

Using the telephone

I need to make a phone call
Tá orm glaoch teileafóin a dhéanamh
Taw urm glayokh tellafone ah yannoo

What is the code for America?
Céard é an cód diailithe faoi choinne Mheiriceá?
Kerd ay un kowde dee-awlihha fwee khon-ye verikaw

I would like to make a reversed charge call
Ba mhaith liom glaoch a chur le malairt táillí
Buh wah lyum glayock ah khur le mollirch tawlee

The number I need is...
Is í .... an uimhir atá uaim
Ishee .... un ivvir ataw woo-im

What is the charge?
Cad é an táille?
Kad ay un tawlyeh

Please, call me back
Glaoigh ar ais orm le do thoil
Glee er ash urm leh duh hull

I am sorry. We were cut off
Tá brón orm. Chlis ar an líne
Taw brone urm. Khlis air an leena

197

What you may hear

What you may hear

The number is out of order
Ní oibríonn an uimhir sin
Nee ibree-on an ivvir shin

The líne is engaged (busy)
Tá an líne gnóthach
Taw un leena g'now-hakh

I am trying to connect you
Tá mé ag iarraidh tú a chur tríd
Taw may egg eerree too a khur treedj

Please go ahead
Lean ar aghaidh le do thoil
Lan er eye-ig leh duh hull

Hello, this is the manager
Dia duit, seo an bainisteoir / Dia duit, an bainisteoir ag caint
Dee-ah ditch, shoh un banishtore / Dee-ah ditch, un bonishtore egg kanch

I am putting you through to Mr O' Hara
Tá mé do do chur tríd chuig an Uasal Ó hEara
Taw may doh doh khur treedj higg un ooasal oh hara

I cannot obtain this number
Níl mé in ann an uimhir seo a fháil
Neel may in unn un ivvir shoh ah awl

Changing money

Ireland's currency is the euro (€). All banks will have a Bureau de change where you can change your money. You will also be able to change your money at the airport, or in foreign exchange centres, but this may be more expensive in terms of commission. You will have no problems exchanging sterling for euro and vice versa, and no problems with other major currencies. If you wish to buy the currency of countries that are not typical holiday destinations you should give the bank a week's notice. Similarly, if you wish to buy more than €1000 of another currency, you should give the bank a few day's notice.

Has my cash arrived?
Ar tháinig mo airgead tirim go fóill?
Er hawnig muh arrigid tirrim guh fowle

I would like to obtain a cash advance with my credit card
Ba mhaith liom airgead tirim a fháil le mo chárta creidmheasa
Buh wah lyum arrigid tirrim ah awl leh muh khorta kredjvassa

This is the name and address of my bank
Seo é ainm agus seoladh mo bhainc
Shoh ay annim oggus showla muh vank

Changing money

Can I change these traveller's cheques?
An bhféadfainn na seiceanna turasóra seo a bhriseadh?
Un vayd-finn nah sheckinna tura-sore-ah shoh ah vrisha

Can I change these notes (bills)?
An bhféadfainn na nótaí seo a bhriseadh?
Un vayd-finn nah nowtee shoh ah vrisha

Here is my passport
Seo é mo phas
Shoh ay muh fass

What is the rate of exchange?
Céard é an ráta malairte?
Kerd ay un rawta mollircha

What is the rate for — sterling?
Céard é an ráta malairte — don phunt Sasanach?
Kerd ay un rawta mollircha — dun funt Sassanakh

— dollars?
Céard é an ráta malairte — don dollar?
Kerd ay un rawta mollircha — dun dollar

What is your commission?
Céard é an coimisiún atá uait?
Kerd ay un komishoon ataw woo-it

HEALTH

Everyone in Ireland can speak English so English speakers will be able to be understood in an emergency situation without need of this phrasebook! If you need to visit a doctor or visit a hospital, visitors to Ireland who hold a European Health Insurance Card (EHIC), are entitled to free treatment in Health Service Executive and voluntary hospitals. UK and CTA (Common Travel Area) citizens do not require an EHIC.

What's wrong?

I need a doctor
Tá orm dochtúir a fheiceáil
Taw urm dokh-ture ah eckawl

Can I see a doctor?
An bhféadfainn dochtúir a fheiceáil?
Un vayd-finn dokh-ture ah eckawl

He/she is hurt
Tá sé/sí gortaithe
Taw shay/shee gurtehha

What's wrong?

He/she has been badly injured
Gortaíodh sé/sí go dona
Gurtee-oo shay/shee guh dunna

He/she has burnt himself/herself
Dhóigh sé/sí é/í féin
Ghow-ay shay/shee ay/ee fayne

He/she has dislocated his / her shoulder
Chuir sé/sí a ghualainn/a gualainn as alt
Khur shay/shee ah ghoo-ahlinn/a goo-ahlinn ass alt

He/she is unconscious
Tá sé/sí gan aithne
Taw shay/shee ahh-nyeh

He/she has a temperature
Tá fiabhras ard air/uirthi
Taw fee-avrass ard air/urhee

He/she has been bitten
Baineadh greim as/aisti
Bwin-yoo grem ass/as-tchee

My son has cut himself
Ghearr mo mhac é féin
Gh'yarr muh wak ay fayne

My son is ill
Tá mo mhac tinn
Taw muh wak teen

What's wrong?

I am ill
Tá mé tinn
Taw may teen

I am a diabetic
Is diabaetach mé
Iss dee-abaytakh may

I am allergic to penicillin
Tá ailéirge phinisilin agam
Taw awlergeh finisilin agum

I am badly sunburnt
Tá mé griandóite go dona
Taw may greendowtcha guh dunna

I am constipated
Tá iatacht orm
Taw ee-ahtakht urm

I cannot sleep
Ní féidir liom codladh
Nee fay-djir lyum kulla

I feel dizzy
Tá meadhrán i mo cheann
Taw m'yowrawn ih mu khyun

I feel faint
Mothaím lag
Muhee-um lag

203

What's wrong?

I feel nauseous
Tá masma orm
Taw masma urm

I fell
Thit mé
Hitch may

I have a pain here
Tá pian agam anseo
Taw pee-an agum unshoh

I have a rash here
Tá gríos orm anseo
Taw grees urm unshoh

I have been sick
Bhí mé tinn
Vee may teen

I have been stung
Cuireadh cealg ionam
Kwirroo k'yalg unnum

I have cut myself
Ghearr mé mé féin
Ghyarr may may fayne

I have diarrhoea
Tá buinneach orm
Taw bwinyakh urm

What's wrong?

I have pulled a muscle
Tharraing mé matán
Harrang may matan

I have sunstroke
Tá goin ghréine orm
Taw gowyn ghraynyeh urm

I suffer from high blood pressure
Bíonn brú ard fola agam
Bee-onn broo ard fulla agum

I think I have food poisoning
Ceapaim gur ith mé bia truaillithe
K'yapam gur ihh may bee-ah troo-awlihha

It is inflamed here
Tá sé athlasta ansco
Taw shay ahh-lasta unshoh

My arm is broken
Tá mo lámh briste
Taw muh lawve brishta

My stomach is upset
Tá mo bholg tinn
Taw muh wulg teen

My tongue is coated
Tá mo theanga faoi choirt
Taw muh h'yanga fwee khwirt

205

What's wrong?

There is a swelling here
Tá at anseo
Taw at unshoh

    I have hurt — my arm
Ghortaigh mé — mo lámh
Ghurtee may — muh lawve

        — my leg
Ghortaigh mé — mo chos
Ghurtee may — muh khus

           It is painful — to walk
Tá sé pianmhar nuair a — shiúlaim
Taw shay peenwar noor ah — hyoolam

                — to breathe
Tá sé pianmhar nuair a — tharraingím anáil
Taw shay peenwar noor ah — harrang-eem anal

                — to swallow
Tá sé pianmhar nuair a — shlogaim
Taw shay peenwar noor ah — luggam

I have a headache
Tá tinneas cinn orm
Taw tchinnass keen urm

I have a sore throat
Tá scornach tinn orm
Taw skornakh teen urm

What's wrong?

I have an earache
Tá tinneas cluaise orm
Taw tchinnass kloosheh urm

I am taking these drugs
Tá mé ag tógáil na ndrugaí seo
Taw may egg towgawl na nrugee shoh

Can you give me a prescription for them?
An bhféadfá oideas dochtúra a thabhairt dom chun iad a fháil
Un vayd-faw idyass dukhtoora a hoo-ert dum kun eed ah awl

I am on the pill
Tá mé ag tógáil an phiollaire fhrithghiniúinigh
Taw may egg towgawl un f'yullirra hrih-ghyin-oonee

I am pregnant
Tá mé ag iompar clainne
Taw may egg umpar klinya

My blood group is . . .
Is é . . . mo ghrúpa fola
Iss shay . . . muh ghroopa fulla

I do not know my blood group
Níl mo ghrúpa fola ar eolas agam
Nyeel muh ghroopa fulla er ole-ass agum

I need some antibiotics
Tá frithbheathaigh uaim
Tawn frihh-vahhee woo-am

At the hospital

Do I have to go into hospital?
An bhfuil orm dul isteach san ospidéal?
Un will urm dull iss-chah san uspidjayle

Do I need an operation?
An bhfuil orm dul faoi scian
Un will urm dull fwee shkee-an

At the hospital

Here is my health insurance card (EHIC)
Seo é mo chárta árachais sláinte
Shoh ay muh khorta ore-ahish slawn-cha

How do I get reimbursed?
Conas a bhféadfainn aisíoc a fháil
Kunass ah vayd-finn ashee-ock ah awl

Must I stay in bed?
An bhfuil orm fanacht sa leaba?
Un will urm fanakht sa labba

When will I be able to travel?
Cathain a mbeidh mé ábalta taisteal
Kohhen ah meye may abalta tashtel

Will I be able to go out tomorrow?
An mbeidh mé ábalta dul amach amárach
Un meye may abalta dull amakh amar-akh

Parts of the body

ankle
rúitín
roocheen

arm
lámh
lawve

back
droim
drim

bone
cnámh
knawv

breast
cíoch (mammary) / brollach
kee-akh / brollakh

cheek
grua
groo-ah

chest (internal, for external
see **breast**)
ucht
ukht

ear
cluas
kloo-ass

elbow
uillinn
illin

eye
súil
sool

face
aghaidh
eye

finger
méar
mare

foot
cos
kus

hand
lámh
lawv

Parts of the body

heart
croí
kree

kidney
duán
doo-awn

knee
glúin
gloon

leg
cos
kus

liver
ae
ay

lungs
scámhóga
skaw-owga

mouth
béal
bayl

muscle
matán
matan

neck
muineál
mwin-yayl

nose
srón
srone

skin
craiceann
krackinn

stomach
bolg
bulg

throat
scornach
skornakh

wrist
caol na láimhe
kayl na lie-veh

At the dentist's

I have to see the dentist
Tá orm an fiaclóir a fheiceáil
Taw urm un fee-oklore ah eckawl

I have a toothache
Tá tinneas fiacaile orm
Taw chtinnass feea-kayl-eh urm

Are you going to fill it?
An líonfaidh tú í?
Un leenhee too ee

I have broken a tooth
Bhris mé fiacail
Vrish may feea-kal

Will you have to take it out?
An mbeidh ort í a thógáil amach?
Un meye urt ee ah howgawl amakh

My false teeth are broken
Tá mo chár bréige briste
Taw muh khar bray-gyeh brish-teh

Can you repair them?
An bhféadfá iad a dheisiú?
Un vayd-faw eed ah yeshoo

At the dentist's

My gums are sore
Tá mo dhrandail pianmhar
Taw muh ghrandel peenwar

Please give me an injection
Tabhair instealladh dom le do thoil
Tow-ar inshtalla dum leh duh hull

That hurts
Tá sin pianmhar
Taw shin peenvar

The filling has come out
Thit an líonadh amach
Hitch un leenoo amakh

This one hurts
Tá an ceann seo pianmhar
Taw un k'yowne shoh peenwar

FOR YOUR INFORMATION

Numbers

Numbers can be very complicated in Irish. There are different numbers for counting numbers, things or people.

Counting numbers

When counting aloud, the prefix 'a' is used which puts a 'h' (also known as a seimhiú [*shay-voo*]) before a numeral beginning with a vowel. e.g. a haon = one, a hocht = eight. This prefix is also used in arithmetic, in telling the time, in addresses and in talking about telephone numbers.

This prefix is omitted when specifying a definite number (suim an trí – add the three), or when speaking of a choice of two numbers (trí nó ceathair – three or four).

0	3	6
náid	a trí	a sé
nawje	*a tchree*	*a shay*

1	4	7
a haon	a ceathair	a seacht
a hayne	*a kyehir*	*a shakht*

2	5	8
a dó	a cúig	a hocht
a daw	*a koo-ig*	*a hokht*

Numbers

9
a naoi
a nee

10
a deich
a deh

11
a haon déag
a hayn djayg

12
a dó dhéag
a daw yayg

13
a trí dhéag
a tchree djayg

14
a ceathair déag
a kyehir djayg

15
a cúig-déag
a koo-ig djayg

16
a sé-déag
a shay djayg

17
a seacht-déag
a shakht djayg

18
a hocht-déag
a hokht djayg

19
a naoi-déag
a nee djayg

20
fiche
fihha

21
fiche a haon
fihha a hayne

22
fiche a dó
fihha a daw

23
fiche a trí
fihha a tchree

24
fiche a ceathair
fihha a kyehir

25
fiche a cúig
fihha a koo-ig

26
fiche a sé
fihha a shay

27
fiche a seacht
fihha a shakht

28
fiche a hocht
fihha a hokht

29
fiche a naoi
fihha a nee

30
tríocha
tchree-okha

40
daichead
die-hayd

50
caoga
kayga

Numbers

60
seasca
shasska

70
seachtó
shakhtoe

80
ochtó
okhtoe

90
nócha
no-ha

100
céad
kyayd

200
dhá chéad
ghaw khayd

300
trí chéad
tchree khyayd

400
ceithre chéad
kerra khyayd

500
cúig chéad
koo-ig khyayd

600
sé chéad
shay khyayd

700
seacht gcéad
shakht gayd

800
ocht gcéad
okht gayd

900
naoi gcéad
nee gayd

1000
míle
meela

2000
dhá mhíle
ghaw veela

3000
trí mhíle
tchree veela

4000
ceithre mhíle
kerra veela

10,000
deich míle
deh meela

1,000,000
milliún
mill-yoon

2,000,000
dhá mhilliún
ghaw mhill-yoon

3,000,000
trí mhilliún
tchree mhill-yoon

Numbers

Counting things

When using a number before a noun, numbers can appear differently and the noun following a number is always singular, although exceptions do exist which will be explained later.

Below is an example of the counting of nouns by counting coats, the Irish for which is *cóta*. Note the differences in the spelling of *cóta*.

1 coat	**6 coats**	**11 coats**
cóta amháin	sé chóta	aon cóta déag
kota awine	*shay khota*	*ayne khota djayg*
2 coats	**7 coats**	**12 coats**
dhá chóta	seacht gcóta	dhá chóta déag
ghaw khota	*shakht gota*	*ghaw khota djayg*
3 coats	**8 coats**	**13 coats**
trí chóta	ocht gcóta	trí chóta déag
tchree khota	*okht gota*	*tchree khota djayg*
4 coats	**9 coats**	**14 coats**
ceithre chóta	naoi gcóta	ceithre chóta déag
kerra khota	*nee gota*	*kerra khota djayg*
5 coat	**10 coats**	**15 coats**
cúig chóta	deich gcóta	cúig chóta déag
koo-ig khota	*deh gota*	*koo-ig khota djayg*

16 coats
sé chóta déag
shay khota djayg

18 coats
ocht gcóta déag
okht gota djayg

20 coats
fiche gcóta
fihha cota

17 coats
seacht gcóta déag
shakht gota djayg

19 coats
naoi gcóta déag
nee gota djayg

21 coats
aon chóta is fiche
ayne khota is fihha

As you can see, numbers 2 to 6 and 12 to 16 are spelt with an added 'h' after their first letter. This is known as a *séimhiú* (*shay-voo*). Séimhiú can be used in many grammatical contexts, but the rules explained here only pertain to their use in association with numbers. A séimhiú is added to nouns which come after the numbers containing the numbers 2 - 6, whether it be 2, 12, 22, 32 etc. A séimhiú cannot be added to nouns beginning with vowels and only to nouns beginning with the following consonants: b, c, d, f, g, m, p, s, t.

2 needles (biorán)
dhá bhiorán
ghaw virrawn

4 drinks (deoch)
ceithre dheoch
kerra yawkh

6 gates (geata)
shay gheata
shay gh'yata

3 tables (tábla)
trí thábla
tchree habla

5 saucers (fochupán)
cúig fhochupán
koo-ig ow-khupan

2 fingers (méar)
dhá mhéar
ghaw vayr

Numbers

3 pens (peann)
trí pheann
tchree fann

5 wells (tobar)
cúig thobar
koo-ig hubber

6 bulls (tarbh)
cúig tharbh
koo-ig haroo

4 shops (siopa)
ceithre shiopa
kerra h'yuppa

Numbers 7 to 10, 17 to 19 are also changed, spelt with a 'g' at the beginning of the word. This is an *urú* (*uroo*). An urú is added to the beginning of nouns, and a different urú is used for nouns beginning with different letters.

Nouns beginning with vowels take 'n-' as an urú; 'm' is used as an urú for nouns beginning with 'b'; 'g' is the urú for 'c'; 'n' is the urú for 'd' and 'g'; 'bh' is the urú for 'f'; 'b' is the urú for 'p'; and 'd' is the urú for 't'. Nouns beginning with other letters will not take an urú.

7 donkeys (asal)
seacht n-asal
shakht nassal

10 hotels (óstán)
deich n-óstan
dehh nostawn

9 coats (cóta)
naoi gcóta
nee gota

8 birds (éan)
ocht n-éan
okht nyayne

7 apples (úll)
seacht n-úll
shakht noo-ill

10 drinks (deoch)
deich ndeoch
dehh nyawkh

9 fish (iasc)
naoi n-iasc
nee nee-ask

8 needles (biorán)
ocht mbiorán
okht mirrawn

7 seagulls (faoileán)
seacht bhfaoileán
shakht vwaylayn

8 gates (geata)
ocht ngeata
okht n'yata

9 pens (peann)
naoi bpeann
nee bann

10 wells (tobar)
deich dtobar
dehh dubber

Multiples of ten (like *daichead* – 40, *caoga* – 50) are single words and have no effect on the following noun. The numbers after 20 follow the same rules of séimhiú and urú, but are written as follows.

20 glasses
fiche gloine
fihha gliyn-yeh

22 glasses
dhá ghloine is fiche
ghaw ghliyn-yeh is fihha

21 glasses
aon ghloine is fiche
ayne ghliyn-yeh is fihha

27 glasses
seacht ngloine is fiche
shakht ngliyn-yeh is fiche

The numbers 21, 22 and 27 are given here as examples. Expect all of the numbers after this to follow a similar pattern.

As I have said, when counting nouns, one does not use the noun's plural, and the numbers 2 to 6 take séimhiú and the numbers 7 to 10 take urú. However, the following nouns exist as exceptions. Here are the difference which one encounters when dealing with these numbers:

219

Numbers

bliain, *bleen*, year

2	3–6	7–10
bhliain	bliana	mbliana

ceann, *k'yowne*, head/ one of

2	3–6	7–10
cheann	cinn	gcinn

uair *oor*, instance/hour

2	3–6	7–10
uair	huaire	n-uaire

orlach, *orlok*, inch

2	3–6	7–10
orlach	horlaí	n-orlaí

troigh, *trow*, foot (measurement)

2	3–6	7–10
throigh	troithe	dtroithe

pingin, *pingin*, penny

2	3–6	7–10
phingin	pingine	bpingine

seachtain, *shokten*, week

2	3–10
sheachtain	seachtaine

Counting people

There is a different set of numbers for counting people and personal nouns. These numbers can qualify a personal noun or stand alone. For example one can say *triúr* – three people; or *triúr mac* – three sons; or *ceathrar dlíodóirí* – four lawyers.

Numbers

1	**5**	**9**
duine amháin	cúigéar	naíonúr
dinna awine	*koo-ig-ar*	*neenur*
2	**6**	**10**
beirt	seisear	deichniúr
bertch	*sheshar*	*dehnur*
3	**7**	**11**
triúr	seachtar	duine déag
troor	*shakhtar*	*dinna dayg*
4	**8**	**12**
ceathrar	ochtar	beirt déag
kyahrar	*okhtar*	*berch dayg*

For numbers of people higher than twelve, the ordinary system of numbering nouns is used: 13 people is *trí dhuine dhéag*, etc.

Unlike the counting of other nouns, plurals are used and the *séimhiú* is only used after the number two, *beirt*, and only in the case of nouns beginning with the following consonants: b, c, f, g, m, p.

2 boys (buachaill)
beirt bhuachaillí
berch vookallee

2 farmers (feirmeoir)
beirt fheirmeoirí
berch ermyore-ee

12 girls (cailín)
beirt chailíní déag
berch kholleenee dayg

12 policemen (garda)
beirt ghardaí déag
berch ghordee dayg

221

Days

2 teachers (múinteoir)
beirt mhúinteoirí
berch voonchore-ee

12 children (páiste)
beirt pháistí déag
berch fawshtee dayg

Days

Sunday
An Domhnach/Dé Domhnaigh
An down-akh / djay down-ee

Thursday
Déardaoin
Djare-deen

Monday
An Luan/Dé Luain
An loon/djay Looin

Friday
An Aoine/Dé hAoine
An eena/djay heena

Tuesday
An Mháirt/Dé Máirt
An warch/djay Vorch

Saturday
An Satharn/Dé Sathairn
An sahharn/djay Sahharn

Wednesday
An Chéadaoin/Dé Céadaoin
An khaydeen/djay kaydeen

Dates

on Friday
ar an Aoine
air un eena

last Tuesday
Dé Máirt seo caite
djay march shoh katcha

next Tuesday
dé Máirt seo chugainn
Djay march shoh hugginn

yesterday
inné
Inn-yay

Times of the year

today
inniu
inn-yoo

tomorrow
amárach
amar-akh

in June
I Meitheamh
i mehiv

July 7th
An seachtú lá de mhí Iúil
Un shakhtoo law deh vee oo-il

next week
an tseachtain seo chugainn
on tchakhtawn shoh huggin

last month
an mhí seo caite
on vee shoh katcha

The seasons

spring
An t- Earrach
un tcharrakh

summer
An Samhradh
un sowrah

autumn
An Fómhar
un fower

winter
An Geimhreadh
un givruh

Times of the year

in spring
san Earrach
san arrakh

in summer
sa Samhradh
sa sowrah

in autumn
san Fhómhar
san ower

in winter
sa Gheimhreadh
sa ghivrah

Months

January Eanáir *anner*	**July** Iúil *oo-il*
February Feabhra *fyowra*	**August** Lúnasa *loonassa*
March Márta *marta*	**September** Méan Fómhair *man fower*
April Aibreán *abrawn*	**October** Deireadh Fómhair *djerra fower*
May Bealtaine *bal-tinyeh*	**November** Samhain *sowin*
June Meitheamh *mehiv*	**December** Nollaig *nullig*

Public holidays and festivals

On public holidays and bank holidays in Ireland, many shops, and all banks will be closed. Large shops and supermarkets will remain open. Ireland's national holiday is St Patrick's

Public holidays and festivals

Day on March 17th. In recent times, St Patrick's day has been celebrated as Patrick's Festival, so expect up to three whole days of events leading up to St Patrick's Day. Other public holiday's are as follows: New Year's Day (January 1st), Easter Monday, May Bank Holiday (first Monday in May), June Bank Holiday (first Monday in June), August Bank Holiday (first Monday in August), Christmas Day (December 25th) and St Stephen's Day (December 26th).

New Year's Day
(January 1)
Lá na bliana úire
la na bleena oora

Epiphany (January 6)
An Eipeafáine
un epahfawna

Saint Brigid's Day
(February 1)
Lá Fhéile Bhríd
law ayla vreej

St Patrick's Day (March 17)
Lá Fhéile Pádraig
law ayla padrig

Good Friday
Aoine an Chéasta
eena un khaysta

Easter
An Cháisc
un khashk

Easter Monday
Luan Cásca
loo-in kawska

May Day
(Labour Day)
Lá Bealtaine
law bal-tinyeh

Midsummer's Eve
Oíche Fhéile Eoin
eeha ayla owen

Midsummer's Day
Lá Fhéile Eoin
law ayla owen

Public holidays and festivals

Christmas Day
(December 25)
Lá Nollag
law nullig

St Stephen's Day,
(December 26)
Lá Fhéile Stiofáin
law ayla stifawn

Lughnasa (harvest festival,
Lammas, August 1)
Lúnasa
loonassa

Puck's Fair (August,
County Kerry)
Aonach Phoic
ayne-ock fwuk

Kilkenny Arts Week
Seachtain na n-Ealaíon, Cill Chainnigh
shokten na nalee-on, kill k'yannee

Lisdoonvarna Matchmaking Festival
Féile Chleamhnais Lios Dún Bhearna
fayla khlownish lisdoonvarna

Adare Jazz Festival
Feis Snagcheoil Áth Dhoire
fesh snogk'yowle aw durra

Cork Jazz Festival
Feis Snagcheoil an Chorcaí
fesh snogk'yowle on khurkee

Feis Ceoil (Classical Music
Festival)
Feis Ceoil
feis k'yowle

Galway Arts Festival
Féile na n-Ealaíon, Gaillimh
fayla na nalee-on, goll-yiv

Galway Oyster Festival
Féile na n-Oisrí, Gaillimh
fayla na nowshree, goll-yiv

226

Colours

black dubh *dooh*	**grey** liath *leeah*
blue gorm *gurim*	**orange** dath oráiste *dah orash-tcheh*
brown donn *dunn*	**pink** bán-dearg *bawn-djarrig*
cream bánbhuí *bawn-wee*	**purple** corcra *korkra*
fawn buídhonn *bweeghun*	**red** dearg *djarrig*
gold dath an óir *dah un ore*	**silver** dath an airgid *dah un arrigidj*
green glas *glass*	**tan** crón *krone*

227

Common adjectives

white bán *bawn*	**red (hair)** rua *roo-ah*
yellow buí *bwee*	**fair (hair)** fionn *finn*

Common adjectives

bad
dona / olc
dunna / ulk

beautiful
álainn
awlinn

big
mór
more

cheap
saor (also means free)
sayr

cold
fuar
foor

expensive
daor / costasach
dayre / kustas-akh

difficult
deacair
djaker

easy
furasta
furasta

fast
gasta
gasta

good
maith
mah

228

Common adjectives

high
ard
ard

hot
te
tcheh

little
beag
byug

long
fada
fadda

new
nua
noo-ah

old
sean
shan

short
gairid
girridj

slow
mall
mal

small
beag
byug

ugly
gránna
grawna

tall
ard
ard

Signs and notices

Signs and notices *(see also Road signs)*

open
ar oscailt
er uskaltch

closed
dúnta
doonta

toilet
leithreas
leh-rass

gentlemen
fir
fir

ladies
mná
mnaw

welcome
fáilte / fáilte romhat
fawl-cha / fawl-cha rowwat

push
uait
woo-it

pull
chugat
huggat

entrance
bealach isteach/slí isteach
bal-akh iss-chah/shlee iss-chah

fire alarm
aláram dóiteáin
alaw-ram do-chawn

ambulance
otharcharr
uhhar-kharr

caution
áire
arreh

lift (elevator)
ardaitheoir
ardee-hore

telephone
teileafón/fón/guthán
tellafone/fone/goohan

Signs and notices

bank
banc
bannk

school
scoil
skull

children crossing
páistí ag trasnú
pash-chee egg trasnoo

police
gardaí
gordee

hospital
ospidéal
uspijayle

poison
nimh
nyiv

lost property office
oifig na mbeart caillte
iffig na mart kyle-cha

travel agency
gníomhaireacht taistil
gneevarockt tash-chill

in case of emergency...
i gcás éigeandála...
i gas aygan-dawla

danger
dáinséar/contúirt
dawnshare/konturch

electricity
leictreachas
leck-trakhas

cashier
airgeadóir
arrigidore

private road
bóthar príobháideach
bowher pree-vaw-jakh

cycle path
cosán rothaíochta
kusawn ruhee-ukhta

no entry
Ná téitear isteach
Naw taytar iss-chah

no thoroughfare
bealach/bóthar dúnta
bal-akh/boe-har doonta

231

Signs and notices

keep off the grass
Ná siúil ar an fhéar
Naw shoo-il air an air

exit
bealach/slí amach
Bal-akh/shlee amah

smoking area
ionad caithimh
onad cah-iv

emergency exit
bealach éalaithe
bal-akh ayle-ihha

smoke free zone
ceantar saor ó thoit
kyantar seer oh hutch

departures
imeachtaí
imakh-tee

no smoking
Ná caitear tobac
Naw catch-er tobak

arrivals
teachtaí
chakh-tee

drinking water
fíoruisce
feerishka

timetable
clár ama
klar ama

baggage
bagáiste
bagawshta

customs
custaim
kustam

information
eolas
ole-ass

litter
bruscar
brusker

232

Signs and notices

no picture taking
cosc ar cheamairí
kosk er khamerree

souvenirs
cuimhneacháin
kivnahine

no admission charge
saorchead isteach
sayor-khyad iss-chah

sale
reic
wreck

price list
luachliosta
looakh-lista

reserved
in áirithe
in ore-ihha

for sale
ar díol
er deeoll

to let
ar cíos
er keeoss

special offer
tairiscint speisialta
tarishkint spesheelta

employees only
fostaithe amháin
fusteehha awine

In an Emergency

What to do

If you witness a crime, a fire or an accident you should call 112, or 999. The emergency call is free from any phone. Once you are connected to an operator you should clearly state which service you require: Police, Fire Brigade, Ambulance or Coast Guard.

If you happen to be a victim of a crime that needs reporting go straight to the nearest police station, police stations in the Republic of Ireland will be marked Garda.

Should you need to be admitted to the emergency ward of a hospital your needs will be dealt with free of charge if you are an EU citizen. If not from the UK, make sure to present your EHIC card. If you are in an emergency situation it will be necessary to get your point across as clearly and quickly as possible, so it is advised you speak English to emergency personnel. These phrases are mostly intended for your information only.

What to do

Call — the fire brigade
Cuir fios ar an — mbriogáid dóiteáin
Kur fiss er on — mbrigawje dough-chawn

Call — the police
Cuir fios ar na — Gardaí
Kur fiss er nah — Gordee

— an ambulance
Cuir fios ar an — otharcharr
Kur fiss er un — uhharkhorr

Get a doctor
Cuir fios ar an dochtúir
Kur fiss er un dukhtoor

There is a fire
Tá tine ann
Taw tinna unn

Where is — the British consulate?
Cá bhfuil — Consalacht na Breataine?
Kaw will — konsalokht nah bratanya

— the police station?
Cá bhfuil — Stáisiún na nGardaí?
Kaw will — Stawshoon nah nordee